LOVE BIG

LOVE **BIG**

The Power of Revolutionary Relationships to Heal the World

Rozella Haydée White

Fortress Press

Minneapolis

TABLE OF CONTENTS

This dedication is really long, and I'm not even going to apologize for it. It is what it is because relationships form the core of who I am. I would not be who I am nor would I have written this book without the support and love of so many people—without these revolutionary relationships.

To the women who came before me: Rose Ella, the granddaughter of sharecroppers; Haydée Gisela, the daughter of Spanish-speaking Afro-Caribbean migrants; and Diane Frances, the one who first embodied revolutionary relationships. These are the grandmothers and mother who modeled love big.

To the generation coming after me, Jaden Isaiah and Brooklyn Roze, the nephew and niece that I love with all of my heart. I want to make this world a more loving place for you. Remember to always love big.

To my mother, my father, my brother (Diane, Clarence, Cole), the foundation of who I am and how I love today. My family has had our share of trials and tribulations, but we continue to practice revolutionary relationships with each other and have committed to love big.

To the Mo. City Divas (Stephanie, Nu'Nicka, Shannon, Kellee, Rachel), my childhood sisters who "knew me when." We grew from girls to grown-ass women who value honesty, loyalty, and a deep and abiding love of God, self, and family. You helped me become, and our relationships led me to love big.

To my Soul Sisters (Beth, Leila, Jen, Andrea, Brittany, Amber, Karin); I wish for every woman to have women in their lives like the ones I have in mine. I wish for everyone to experience women who have covenanted to be in revolutionary relationships, being there for each other in the face of all that life brings. When others disappear, my Soul Sisters remain. They spoil me with their love. They always have my back. They call me out on my shit. They remind me to never play small and to go after every dream I have. These women have shown me that I will never be alone and continually remind me of my belovedness. They love big at all times and in all ways.

To my Peeps (Andrea, Tuhina, Jason); we came together for the United Nations Commission on the Status of Women in 2015. We've stayed together because of our deep love for one another, our common experiences with depression and anxiety, our unrelenting pursuit of justice, and our love of liquor. You love me big, and I am always reminded of who I was created to be through our revolutionary relationships.

To the Hedge (Nadia, Neichelle, Jes, Rachel, Nichole, Winnie, Mihee, Emily, Jeff, Kerlin, Austin, Jodi); you always need people in your life who push you to the next level not just mentally but also emotionally and spiritually. Our vocations brought us together, and the Divine Feminine keeps us connected. I figured out that I could be both wild and holy because of you. The Hedge breathes life into me and embodies divine love without apology.

To my brothers from other mothers (Brady, Chris, Jonathan, Eubie, Yehiel, Shawn), the men in my life who show me unconditional love and support; men who model for me what loving relationships look like with their partners, their mothers, and their children; men who are in touch with their vulnerability; men who love big, without shame.

To my mentors (Peggy, Angela, Hazel, Mary, Reesheda); these are the people who impart their time, wisdom, and resources on my life. They make it a point to speak life to me, at all times, and empower me to be the woman leader I am today.

To the Lovers (unnamed). You've taught me the most important lesson of all. If I don't love myself first, then I'm not loving big. In the words of Ariana Grande, thank you, next.

FOREWORD

I grabbed my phone, some headphones, and my Great
Dane and bolted out the front door into the bright Colo-
rado sun before I totally lost it. I was in the middle of
the worst part of writing a book—the part where you
are sure you are a miserable fraud who will never pull
off such a scam. The part where you have no idea how
to say what you have in your heart. The part where you
stare at a blank computer screen for days on end and
try to convince yourself it counts as writing. My confi-
dence was shot, and I was sure that I had taken on the
impossible.

Zacchaeus pulled at the leash. I changed the play-
list on my phone to something angry and quickened
my pace, hoping to pound out the insecurity in my
head with the quickness in my feet. Halfway through

Nirvana's "Smells Like Teen Spirit," my phone rang. I swiped right to answer, because it was Rozella.

You see, Rozella has what I lack: an unwavering faith in me. As you read this book and see that she says that she believes in people, I am here to say that it is true. To be in a relationship with Rozella is to be loved and loved big.

"I get that you feel this way, Nadia," she said with her typical conviction and warmth, "but it's just a feeling. And you know what's bigger than feelings? *Truth.* And the *truth* is that God would not call you and then fail to equip you. I promise that you already have access to everything you need."

When she then asked if she could pray for me over the phone, my reply was, "Fuck you for making me cry in public, Roze! I mean . . . yes, please."

When Rozella speaks into someone's life, she draws on a source that is not just her; she draws from *the* source. Her blessings and prayers over others come from the heart of God, as if she can reach into our created place, the place in us that is connected to the one from whom we came, the place in us that still hums with the vibration of a mother God's song to her beloved babe-in-arms. Rozella's relationships are revolutionary. She is a world-class encourager, but not the bullshit tell-you-what-you-want-to-hear-so-you-will-like-them kind. She is the tell-you-what-you-need-to-hear-because-this-bankrupt-world-has-stolen-our-original-song-from-us kind. When she says something encouraging, I believe her. You can, too. And sometimes she makes you cry when you're walking through your very own neighborhood even though you hate that kind of public vulnerability. And sometimes her loving, healing, and true words empower you to actually do the impossible. And then you go back home, hang up the dog's leash, and get back to work.

Enjoy my friend Rozella. But keep some tissues handy.

Nadia Bolz-Weber

INTRODUCTION

If we have no peace it's because we have
forgotten that we belong to each other.
—Mother Teresa

The Shrinking Roze

I haven't always been the woman that I am today. I was
an incredibly shy child, more comfortable with a book
than with people. Books were my security blanket—they
were always with me, providing comfort and spurring
on my imagination. I loved romance books, mysteries, and young-adult stories of people coming to know
themselves and each other. I would try to leave group
gatherings early or rush to finish assignments, always
looking for an excuse to pull out a book and get lost in
a story.

Looking back, I realize that my love of books had a
lot to do with feeling like I didn't belong. I wasn't comfortable in my skin and was unsure of myself. I was

an awkward child, and public spaces, including school, were terrifying. People could be so mean, and I was so sensitive. I've learned that I'm an empath, but as a child, the world was a difficult place to inhabit. So many emotions ran through me, including those I could sense simply by being near others. At times, it was all too much.

Books were my refuge and constant companion during the ups and downs of my childhood. They provided an escape from the conflict in my family and other things I could not control. The stories I encountered lifted my spirit and helped me realize that I was not alone. They expanded my views of people from different backgrounds and shared with me the beauty of other lands and cultures. Books opened me up to a different way of thinking and led me to begin the journey of self-discovery. More than anything, books lifted up a utopic vision for community, for relationships, and for peace. And I have been chasing this vision for most of my life.

We Don't Have Peace

Peace seems like an elusive concept these days. Everywhere I turn, I hear of conflict and destruction. I see people dying and communities being destroyed. The ways people engage one another in public discourse are anything but peaceful. I feel the anxiety and tension rise in my body when I watch cable news or read the latest headlines on Twitter. Whether it's in my home country of the United States or in other countries around the world, I am constantly bombarded by evidence that we are not living in peaceful times. It feels more like pure chaos, like we are riding in a car without a driver and as we try to move forward, we end up going in circles, losing people and parts along the way.

When there is talk of peace, the concept is sorely misunderstood and misused. We romanticize peace, as if it might spontaneously arrive, embodied by people of all colors, ages, identities, abilities, shapes, sizes, languages, and statuses gathered around the proverbial campfire, holding hands, smiling softly at one another, and singing a round of "Kumbaya." But peace is far from this simple, and I grow weary of such saccharine and uncomplicated images of a peaceful future.

It is dangerous to romanticize formidable concepts. Doing so makes them seem weaker, allows us to ignore the long and arduous work needed to bring them about, and removes personal responsibility and collective action from the formula. We are reluctant to take responsibility for all of humanity, and this leads to a continual breakdown of human relationships.

I am just as dubious when I hear people talk about reconciliation in racial-justice conversations. Both of these concepts—peace and reconciliation—require definition before they can be enacted. But there are as many definitions of peace as there are people calling for it. Until we can agree on what we mean by peace—what it looks like and how it should be achieved—we can't begin to make peace a reality.

Think about the phrase "peace in the Middle East." What does that even mean? Does it mean that the United States stops supplying people in the region with weapons? Does it mean that warring populations, many who have been supported and/or undermined by the US government, simply begin to get along? Does it mean that children skip happily down the bombed streets, ignoring the generational trauma and disconnection that has resulted from years of warfare and bloodshed? We don't know what we mean when we say we want peace.

This is also true when it comes to conversations about racial reconciliation. All too often in conversations about racial justice, people jump immediately to talk of reconciliation. No one wants to directly address the harm that has been done. But true reconciliation requires facing hard truths head-on and giving back what was taken from Black and Indigenous people, honoring the labor that built this country and created generational wealth for white Americans. Any other starting point is bullshit and doesn't honor the very people you want to be in relationship with. As a Black woman, I can't name a time when people of color were in life-giving, reciprocal, and uplifting relationships with our white counterparts. This time has never existed, yet we talk about being reconciled as if there is a former reality that we can recreate.

When I talk about peace and reconciliation, I do so relying heavily on my faith. I don't believe that we've experienced true peace and reconciliation yet, but I do believe that both are possible. I have faith in what I cannot yet see but can imagine. People throughout history have had faith in humanity and in something larger than us all. These people helped us set our sights on what could be rather than on what was. We don't just need more people like this today, we also need to remember those who have come before and have inspired humanity to be better, do better, and love better. So when I talk about peace, I'm referring to the peace that one of our prophetic leaders, the Reverend Dr. Martin Luther King Jr., lifted up: "True peace is not merely the absence of tension, but it is the presence of justice."[1]

This changes everything. Peace is not a passive concept but an active one; one that is marked by a movement toward justice. I define justice as equitable access to resources that provide people with the ability and agency to create a life of meaning. Working toward justice requires dismantling any system, ideology, or institution that promotes inequity, divides people according to arbitrary characteristics, and assigns meanings to those characteristics that lead to ongoing oppression. Justice becomes a reality when we recognize that we need one another. When we become justice seekers and peace bearers, we recognize that our lives are inextricably linked. What one person does, thinks, or even believes affects another. We don't live like this is true. And avoiding this truth leads us to the chaos and brokenness we now experience.

We Are Broken

A quick survey of human history shows that humanity has never fully embraced the reality that we belong to each other. Throughout time, different populations have dehumanized other segments of the population in order to build wealth and acquire resources for the sole purpose of consolidating power. This power has then been used as a tool for control. By viewing others as less than human, those in power have justified abuse, oppression, and the literal buying and selling of people.

There are other telltale signs that we are broken and have forgotten that we belong to each other:

- We order our lives in ways that prove that profit matters more than people.
- We turn a blind eye to those suffering in our midst.

- We rationalize the suffering, oppression, and exploitation of others, as if we are not complicit in making this a reality.
- We compartmentalize our public and private lives, as if they are not intertwined and don't impact each other.
- We are more focused on the individual than on the collective.
- We allow for leaders in every sector to get away with spewing hatred, perpetuating violence, and dividing communities.

This way of being has caused deep fractures that allow hatred and division to seep into and infect our lives together. This infection has gone untreated, and we now live with an illness that threatens to overtake us. The symptoms are fear, hatred, and a belief in scarcity. This illness leads us to forget that we belong to each other, and by forgetting this former reality, chaos ensues.

We are not curious about each other. We jump to judgment and are defensive when someone thinks differently. This judgment ignites the spark of fear that's always present. We can no longer see the fear for what it could be—a tool to discern if we are safe or if our livelihood is fundamentally threatened. When this spark becomes a full-blown flame, fear takes over and begins to control every decision, every word, every experience, and every relationship. Fear leads us to turn inward, closing ranks and pushing everyone who is not like us away. This fear serves to further disconnect us from each other. And as we disconnect, hatred springs up.

Hatred forms from a deep self-loathing. When we hate, it's rarely *really* about another person but almost always reflective of something in us that needs restoration. You can always tell when a person doesn't love themselves. It seeps out in hate speech, angry rhetoric, and life-taking commentary. You can't speak life if you are dead inside, if you don't love yourself. When I hear hateful rhetoric or witness hateful behavior, I immediately wonder what happened to that person to lead to such a profound disconnection from those around them and, ultimately, from themselves. When we hate another, we fail to recognize their humanity. Hate doesn't just happen. It grows from the spark of fear that is fanned by the belief that there isn't enough for everyone.

Fear and hatred lead to an inevitable conclusion: that there isn't enough. Enough time. Enough resources. Enough jobs. Enough money. Enough joy. Enough love. This belief in scarcity is the biggest sign that we don't believe that we belong to each other—leading to the absence of peace and a world of chaos.

All Is Not Lost. Healing Is Possible.

Despite all our brokenness, I believe that healing is possible. I have hope for a new reality; for a world and for relationships that reflect a sense of belonging. I believe that in spite of the ways it has been used to oppress, faith has the power to heal us. Not just any faith, however, but a faith that is creative, liberative, and sustaining; faith that is reflective of the ultimate lover, God. This faith has the power to heal us. I believe that a faith that is embodied in relationship has the power to make us well.

This faith begins with a story of an imaginative God who created all things and named them as good. Before any of us were created, this God existed as an entity already in relationship with Godself, and this relationship teaches us how to be in relationships with others. This God is a lover who creates, liberates, and sustains creation. The creation story shows a God who lovingly formed every aspect of creation. All you have to do is look at nature in its various forms to see the work of a God who has Divine imagination and who loves big. After each part of our world was created, God made a proclamation, "It is good."

At the end of the creation story, God created humanity. Not only did God repeat the words "it is good," but God did something with humanity that didn't happen with the other aspects of creation. In us, in humans, God created beings who are a direct reflection of God. We are created in the image of God. This means that if God is the ultimate lover, we are also lovers. We were created in relationship—to be cocreators, to be liberators, to be sustainers, all because God created us in God's very own Divine image. In creation, God shows us what it looks like to belong to each other, to be in a relationship that is life-giving and reflective of the abundant nature of God and God's creation.

All of creation interacts with itself to form a world that produces what it needs to thrive. Faith leads us to remember our story—who we belong to and who we are. This faith moves us to reorder our relationships, to nurture our relationship with the Divine, which leads us to fall in love with ourselves and with others. This love leads us back to God, moving us deeper into God's promise of abundance. This faith invites us to recreate a world where we do belong to each other and justice becomes a way of life. Anytime we think that there isn't enough, we have stopped believing the creation story. We have forgotten that God created a world full of everything we need. God didn't create us to simply survive. God created us to thrive. When we are fearful, we become disconnected from ourselves and from each other. This disconnection breeds hatred and leads us to live with a scarcity mindset.

Faith as a cure is powerful because it's holistic. It doesn't just address our brokenness; it addresses the conditions that led to the weakening of humanity to begin with. Our healing starts with reconnecting to God holistically. We then fall in love with our entire being— mind, heart, body, and soul. Our minds are roused as we consider what formed us and as we turn our judgment into curiosity so we can be open to learning new ways of being. Our broken hearts are repaired, and we attend to our feelings, recognizing that everything can be redeemed. Our bodies are reformed as we address limiting beliefs about our physical forms and the bodies of others, recognizing that we are made in the image of God. Our souls are restored as we learn to trust the inner voice of wisdom and follow her lead.

Faith leads us to recreate our world and engage in *revolutionary relationships* with ourselves and with others. Revolutionary relationships are *life-giving, risk-taking, vulnerable, gracious, forgiving, and diverse, and hold us accountable.* Revolutionary relationships provide additional healing. Revolutionary relationships powered by love can heal the brokenness of our individual and collective lives. Revolutionary relationships that cross dividing lines of race, gender, religion, orientation, ability, identity, and class can provide relief. Revolutionary relationships can usher us into a reality marked by faith, connection, and a belief in abundance that combats fear, hatred, and a belief in scarcity. Revolutionary relationships can bring us back to center, back to the original goodness and wholeness that the Creator intended for her creation. Revolutionary relationships continue to call us out and lead us back to each other, mirroring the cycle of life. When we come back to the beginning, we come back to the place where healing and connection are found.

We have experienced glimpses of healing. Think, for example, of how we come together after a tragedy. I'll never forget the love that poured out after 9/11. Yes, some undertook retaliatory and hateful actions, but so many people shared their homes, their time, and their love with strangers in need of support.

I live in Houston, and in August 2017, we were hit by Hurricane Harvey, which devastated our city and its inhabitants. Texans are a strong and fiercely loving bunch. People rescued folks who were stranded by rising waters. Volunteers poured out in record numbers to provide material assistance and staff shelters. Friends of mine loaned me their car for over a week after my car flooded. They didn't ask for anything in return and let me know that the car was mine to use for as long as I needed it.

Many of us have supported an online fundraiser for a family in need, for those who have been impacted by major health issues or death and are in need of financial assistance. These are glimpses of us acting as though we belong to one another, but these actions tend to be in response to something bad happening. What if we practiced the belief that we belong to one another daily? What if we didn't wait until the proverbial shit hit the fan before we poured out ourselves for one another?

Healing doesn't happen overnight. It requires ongoing care and attention. Just when we think we are healed, something happens that can lead us back into ourselves, making us believe the lie of scarcity and taking us off course. Knowing something and believing something are very different than living something. No matter how much we know, this knowledge doesn't always translate into action. I know what I need to do to be healthy: I need sleep, exercise, spiritual grounding, meaningful relationships, and sun. And yet, I find myself time and time again ignoring what I know to be true in favor of anything and everything else. I can list a multitude of reasons why I don't take the time to care for myself, but they often amount to no more than excuses. Just because I know better doesn't mean I do better. Much like the way humanity comes together in the face of tragedy, my behavior tends to change when I'm faced with the news that something serious is happening with my health. This becomes my impetus for putting knowledge into action. I often wonder if I could save myself, my doctors, and even God the frustration if I just practiced knowledge from the get-go.

We have forgotten the beginning of our story. We have forgotten, or never believed, that we were crafted in the Divine's image to be lovers—to love big and to practice this love with ourselves and with each other. We know we are on a journey toward healing when we remember that we belong to each other. When we are healed, we create new, life-giving realities; liberate ourselves and others from systems, ideologies, and structures that are oppressive; and sustain one another to live lives of peace marked by justice. This is how we love big, and this leads us to love despite differences, to love in the face of hardships and despair, to love ourselves and others deeply and passionately, to love in ways that change us all.

CHAPTER 1

Faith in God as a Lover

Now faith is the substance of things hoped
for, the evidence of things not seen.
—Hebrews 11:1 KJV

Roze-Tinted Glasses

I was often called naïve as a child because I chose to believe the best in people or hoped for outcomes that benefited everyone. I was always optimistic, believing that things and people would work out for the good. I never thought this was a bad thing until I was labeled naïve and ridiculed for not knowing the "ways of the world." This taught me early on that I was different. I came to understand that many people are pessimistic, not believing that good really outweighs evil or that humanity can rise to the occasion and care for each other. In their defense, I recognize that this pessimism comes from lived experience. When you have been on the receiving end of trauma or have witnessed evil in your day-to-day existence, it becomes almost impossible to believe that good can overcome all of the brokenness.

My father used to say that I viewed the world through rose-tinted glasses. He always said this with a condescending tone—"oh, my poor, sweet baby, believing the best in everyone"—but I found it to be quite accurate as my nickname is Roze (pronounced *rose*) and I wear glasses. And I do view the world through lenses that are unique to me. Viewing the world through Roze-tinted glasses means that I look at my environment, people, and cultures with an air of curiosity and a belief that people ultimately are good. And when I say good, I don't mean overly moral or always right-acting or perfect. I don't know anyone who actually falls into any of those categories, and if I did I think we'd struggle to relate to one another. When I say that I believe that people are ultimately good, I mean that people sincerely want the best for themselves and those they care about, that in the face of trauma or disaster, people will show up for others offering support and resources. Viewing the world through Roze-tinted glasses means that I ultimately have faith in humanity and trust that all manner of things will be made well.

Believing people and having faith in them is foundational to who I am. When I talk about faith, it's with the conviction that because people are made in the image of God, then they are worthy of my faith. I believe people and I believe *in* people. Humans have an immense capacity to hurt others, but we also have an incredible ability to love each other. We are resilient, constantly transforming the shit of our lives into fertilizer that has the power to heal us, individually and collectively. This makes me respect and love people even more. When confronted with someone who views the world differently than I do, especially if they lean toward pessimism, I often wonder about the shit of their life. I wonder what has led them to see the world and her inhabitants in mistrustful ways. I truly want to know what has led to their lack of faith in others. In these moments, I put on my Roze-tinted glasses and view them with love and curiosity. None of us are the way we are without cause. Our lives, our experiences, our relationships, and any number of things out of our control impact how we view ourselves, others, and the world. We lean into faith when we practice more grace and patience with ourselves and one another, turning our judgments into curiosity.

We are experiencing a crisis of faith—not just in others, but in ourselves. Our pessimism is at an all-time high, and honestly, why wouldn't it be? People are struggling to make ends meet, working hard and not seeing a return on their efforts. Communities are being broken apart, and everyone seems to be out for themselves. Our political discourse is more fragmented and divisive than ever. Our religious communities are floundering. Joy is hard to come by, as we never seem to get relief from our struggles and heartbreaks. All of this, along with a lack of faith that things can be any different, contributes to our brokenness. We are in need of healing. My Roze-tinted glasses lead me to be believe that healing is absolutely possible, but it can be hard to come by. Distrust of those around us keeps us from being made well.

The first step toward healing is to reclaim our faith. To love big is to have faith in yourself, in others, and in God—a faith that is creative, liberating, and sustaining, without condition. To love big is to have faith, even when you don't understand how faith works and especially when you don't believe that faith even matters. To love big is to trust that another way of being is possible and that this new way has the power to heal us all.

The Beginning of My Faith

I'm not sure when I started to believe that anything is possible and that people are ultimately good. It's not that I haven't experienced trauma and despair in my life, but I somehow have always believed that the present moment isn't the only moment, that there is more to my story and more to others' stories. I credit my outlook on life to my mother and grandmothers. All of them were incredibly faithful women who experienced more heartbreak and brokenness than anyone should experience.

My paternal grandmother was the granddaughter of sharecroppers, one generation removed from slavery. She didn't finish school and was married by the time she was fourteen. She had her first child at fifteen and went on to birth six more children—a total of four boys and three girls. She buried three of her sons before they were twenty-one, each a victim of the heroin epidemic. She buried her oldest daughter, my aunt, who died of cancer a few years ago. My grandmother had one of her legs amputated and now lives with my parents. Her life hasn't been a walk on the beach, and yet, she is one of the most faithful and joyful people I have ever met.

My maternal grandmother buried her mother when she was seven years old and was then raised by three aunts, who were not the nicest women. They migrated from Puerto Rico to New York in the 1920s. These women presented as Black Americans but adamantly identified as Puerto Rican. They did not speak English and were unmarried. These women raised my grandmother and, later, my mother. My grandmother married a childhood family friend and gave birth to my mother within the first year of their marriage. When I got older and did the math, I realized that my grandmother must have been pregnant before they got married, and that the pregnancy likely led to the marriage.

My grandmother and grandfather were never a match and separated shortly after my mother was born. My maternal grandmother was a stalwart in our family and in her faith community. She volunteered her time as a church organist and wrote hymns about God's faithfulness. She gave generously to charity and believed in serving others. She clung to faith and didn't let the circumstances of her upbringing sway her from a belief that life could be beautiful.

My mother was raised by her mother and the aunts after her parents separated. I often wonder what it was like for her as the only child in a house full of women who were known for being a bit difficult. She didn't have a relationship with her father and had no other siblings. I believe these two things drew my mother to my father and to his buoyant and charismatic family. They were the exact opposite of her family, and she was drawn to them like a moth to a flame. My mother met my father when she was in her early twenties, and they began a love affair that resulted in my birth out of wedlock. This caused quite the scandal, and my maternal grandmother tried to convince my mother to have an abortion. My mother was a teacher who risked losing her job because of her "scandalous" status. But my mom persevered. She told me recently that her greatest accomplishment was bringing me to life and that I was a gift that she knew had to be brought into the world. After a separation, a marriage, and a divorce, my mother reconciled with my father. They are together to this day.

These women nurtured faithfulness in my life. Despite their hardships, they continued to live and love and laugh, trusting that there was always more to their story. It's hard not to have faith when I follow in the footsteps of these women. I don't always understand why they stayed strong or how their faith never wavered, but I came to believe that faith is a nonnegotiable, the thing that keeps you alive when everything else around you leads to death. And herein lies the mystery.

The Mystery of Faith

Faith goes deeper than what we feel about someone or something. When I speak of faith, I am referring to the belief that there is more to any moment than what humans can sense. It's not just about what we see, hear, feel, smell, or taste. Faith taps into a sixth sense, a sense that requires us to trust beyond what we can explain or see.

Faith is tricky. It's hard to understand and even harder to explain. It doesn't make logical sense. Run quickly away from any person or institution that tries to rationalize faith or provide simple black-and-white answers for it. An overly rationalized faith is often a judgmental faith, but I want a faith that is open to mystery. Mysteries invite us into the unknown. They leave much to the imagination. Faith beckons us to tap into our creative center and wonder about all the possibilities of any given moment or relationship.

So many people want an absolute. They want situations, experiences, and answers to be cut-and-dried. I understand this desire. Life is hard, and sometimes we just want an easy answer. But I also think that we make life harder by accepting simple answers. When I release my need for things to make sense, I become less defensive and more gracious. The boundaries I've created about who's in and who's out, about what's necessary and what's optional, about what's right and what's wrong, all come tumbling down. The energy that I would expend in keeping things neatly ordered and logical now can be used to hope, connect, and love.

Something happens to people as we age. At some point we receive the message that being an imaginative person who delights in wonder is incompatible with being a responsible, productive adult. As I've gotten older, I've moved further and further away from imagination and childlike wonder. It's no surprise so many are experiencing a crisis of faith. Faith requires us to imagine and to wonder, not just about what could be but about how we are a part of making the world and our relationships better. I've come to view adulthood as *highly* overrated. Our world and our relationships could use more childlike imagination, wonder, and mystery.

I can remember losing hours in books when I was a child. I read so much I would get in trouble for it! I always had a book with me and had no shame in pulling it out if my surrounding company did not stimulate my imagination as much as whatever story I was currently devouring. I would read at restaurants when my parents would take us out with their friends. I read at church when a sermon was particularly boring. I read on road trips. I read under the covers with a flashlight after my mother told me to go to bed. I would even read in school whenever I finished a lesson or when the teacher was no longer holding my interest.

Reading wasn't just an escape for me. It invited me into stories that were full of hope and connection and love. These stories made me believe that life and love—even with all of the ups and downs—could be incredibly uplifting. And at its best, faith invites us to hope, to connect, and to love. Faith beckons us into an alternative world, one that inspires us to believe the unbelievable, connect with ourselves and others, and love deeply and without apology. Faith that is life-giving has the power to hold our deepest desires and hopes. This means that it can inspire trust and lead us to do the seemingly impossible for the purpose of creating a better reality. Faith is strong enough to withstand our questions and doubts. In fact, faith is made stronger when we reflect on the experiences of our life.

At its worst, faith leads to a blind trust, a commitment to something or someone without critique and interrogation. Blind trust leads us to a zombie-like existence. We do what we are told and live a life according to ideals that we have not fully examined simply because the entity we have placed our faith in tells us to. This type of faith doesn't deepen or expand; it becomes stagnant. Without questions and wondering, faith loses its mystery and crosses the dangerous line into the realm of certainty.

Faith takes root in your life—often without logical or rational explanation—for the sole purpose of inviting you to wonder what life could be like if you unapologetically valued and loved yourself, others, and the One who created us all. Faith can lead us to believe in the impossible. It has the power to inspire us to trust the nonsensical and make us believe that extraordinary things can come from an ordinary reality.

This type of faith is a gift. It is something that we are given by a Divine being who has faith in us and wants us to have faith in one another. This faith is deep and wide and all encompassing. It leads us to create and to liberate, and it is sustaining. I am a person who has faith in humanity and in a Divine being because I believe a story that is all about hope and connection and love. This faith beckons us to be the best we can be, as individuals and as a collective of humans who are seeking the best life has to offer.

I choose to believe in a reality that we might catch glimpses of but haven't fully experienced. This faith empowers me because it reminds me that nothing is impossible, even when it hasn't been done or seen before. I believe in a world where justice rolls like an ever-flowing stream. A world where equity is a way of life and all have exactly what they need. A world where people are valued more than profit—where love is the undergirding value—and respect is given to all because our interdependence is acknowledged. This world doesn't yet exist, and yet, I have the audacity of hope. I believe that this world is possible because I believe in something bigger than myself. My faith is rooted in who God is, not in what humanity has or has not done.

In an era where faith is often conflated with certainty, I want to reclaim the mystery of faith. It's not about having the answers but about trusting in something bigger than us all, that something beckoning us deeper and wider is at work. Faith is about looking to our inner wisdom, our senses, our environment, and our relationships for guidance that leads us deeper into what is true. We know we are in the realm of truth when creativity abounds, when liberation is experienced by all, and when our relationships and world are sustained.

Faith is powerful, and I've learned that with great power comes greater responsibility.

The Power of Faith

The faith I speak of is not always present and embodied in the world. The object of our faith and the interpretation of the beliefs that undergird our faith will inform how we embody our faith. What we have faith *in* and how we choose to interpret our belief will inform how we live our faith out.

If a person has faith in material objects, their actions will conspire to protect the material objects present in their life. If a person has faith in finances, they will order their life with a singular focus on attaining more wealth. If a person has faith in power, particularly power over others, their behavior will reflect their desire to be powerful at any cost. Worst of all, I think, is when a person has faith in scarcity, leading them to hoard resources out of the fear that there is not enough for all to be sustained. This belief in scarcity has taken root in many of us, leading us away from each other and from ourselves. Faith in scarcity is deadly, and I don't believe in anything that takes life. I only believe in that which creates life.

When you begin to understand the power of faith, you see how religious extremists pervert faith into something that is only inwardly focused and takes life instead of giving life. I think about the violence that's being done—both literal and theological—in the name of faith. Faith is powerful, and when it's used to stoke the embers of fear, it becomes dangerous. We see this not just among those we label as violent religious extremists but also among everyday people who weaponize faith in order to perpetuate beliefs that divide and oppress.

Faith shouldn't perpetuate fear, it should confront fear and lead us to lean more fully into love, into each other. In our time, faith has been so distorted that it no longer leads us back to each other but heightens our mistrust and gives us reasons to believe the worst about each other. It's time to embrace a faith that brings us closer together.

Faith in God as Lover

There is nothing like being in love—passionate, soul-stirring, life-giving love. I have been head-over-heels in love just a few times in my life. I lost all rational thought and could only think about the other person. I never got enough of their presence. Who they were and how they showed up in the world was absolutely enthralling. Being in love with a person who was also in love with me nurtured my heart. I was able to be my whole self, without worrying that I was too much. I was loved fully and completely. I never had to apologize for who I was or the intensity of my emotions. Love took root in my mind, heart, body, and soul. And it was incredible.

At some point during adulthood, I received messages that this type of love was bad—that it was reckless and wouldn't last. I was advised never to love someone more than they loved me; I should actually find someone who loved me more than I loved them! I was told that the type of love I was seeking wasn't real love because it was too fiery, and fires were all consuming. I could only trust love that was safe and steady. Passion wasn't to be trusted. And so I started to act in ways that weren't authentic to my identity or my desires.

It's taken me almost thirty-seven years, but I call bullshit on all of this advice. Love should be passionate and all consuming. It should lead us to be the best version of ourselves. This doesn't mean that love will make life perfect or that there won't be ups and downs in our relationships. What it means is that true love binds us together, leading us to recognize that we can overcome anything and everything, together.

When I think about God, I think about God as a lover. The faith that I profess is rooted in a belief in a God who loves us deeply, desperately, and with a passion that cannot be contained. This God is always seeking us out, wanting to be with us and wanting us to experience the very best that life has to offer. This God is protective because we are loved so damn much. This God lovingly crafted us in God's own image, so that we reflect God's desires. This God created us to be lovers too.

My faith didn't just spring up out of the blue. The women in my life nurtured it with a particular foundation: they believed in God as a lover. I know this to be true based on how they talked about God, lived their faith, and encouraged me to engage my own relationship with God. They raised me in the Christian tradition, with a particular emphasis on the story of God becoming human in the person of Jesus. This is called the incarnation and is the most passionate act of a God who is desperately in love with humanity: God chose to become human and be with us. The incarnation is proof that God is the ultimate lover.

God wants to be loved in return. Isn't that how the best relationships function? God loves us, and we love God. To be in relationship with God, to have faith in God, is to love God—completely, adoringly, and with all the passion we can muster. Falling more deeply in love with God has taught me more about loving others. Love that is patterned after God's love for us creates, liberates, and sustains us on this journey called life.

The Type of Christian I Am

Then God said, "Let *us* make humankind in *our* image, according to *our* likeness; and let them have dominion over the fish of the sea, and over the birds of the air, and over the cattle, and over all the wild animals of the earth, and over every creeping thing that creeps upon the earth." So God created humankind in his image, in the image of God he created them; male and female he created them.[1]

I believe in a God who exists in three ways, each an entity entirely unto itself yet in constant relationship with the other parts. This particular concept of God is called the Trinity—one God in three persons—and I believe that the Trinity was present at the beginning of creation, that the Trinity actually created creation.

Scholars, religious teachers, philosophers, and leaders throughout the ages have written many commentaries on how the Trinity came to be, how it functions, and why it matters. I am not interested in trying to prove the theory of God as Trinity; I am trying to understand the nature of the relationship that God chooses to live out in the Trinity. Why would God show up within the context of relationship to begin with? What meaning does this hold for me, for my faith, and for my relationships with others?

I want to understand how God the Creator (the parent) relates to God the Liberator (the child) and how God the Liberator relates to God the Sustainer (the spirit). I want to glean all that I can from how God the Creator, Liberator, and Sustainer come together to be GOD. But, let me be clear, I have no desire to prove any of this to you. In fact, a faith that can be proven isn't really faith at all. My goal is to use my faith to add meaning and purpose to my life. Because I believe I am made in the image of this God, I want to delve deeply into those relationships.

I want to be grounded in who I am as an individual and engage in relationships as my truest self, without risking the integrity of who I am. I want my relationships to transform my life and how I relate to others. I want to learn all that I can from what I consider to be the ultimate relationship, the Trinity.

I am a person of Christian faith, one whose faith is rooted in the story of God becoming human. I am interested in the life of God here on earth. I am interested in learning from Jesus's relationships with his family and his inner circle, with those he visited and those he healed. I am interested in how Jesus nurtured a relationship with Godself and how his self-understanding led to understanding others.

I believe in a God who is a relationship unto Godself. I happen to believe the ridiculous story of a Divine being who hovered over the earth before anything was on it or in it. This being formed all that we know to be creation. The same Creator chose to leave their Divine realm to become human. This fully human and fully Divine being lived an incredible life, died a heartbreaking death, and came back to life. A promise was made to humanity that this Divine being would not leave us but send an advocate who would be with us all, every step of the way. This advocate is known to be the Holy Spirit, the breath of life that was imparted on us all and is a constant presence of the Divine in our daily lives. The only way to believe something as unbelievable as this is to have faith.

I believe in this story because I have experienced it as life-giving. Belief in an incarnational God has transformed my life for the better. I have witnessed how this story has changed other people's lives, too. The life-giving nature of this story gives birth to new creations—new people—who are moved to justice and have more compassion, more humility, and more love.

The Type of Christian I Am Not

Defining terms is really important, especially in a time such as this. Christianity has been co-opted by people who don't represent me and those like me. I sometimes cringe when I'm introduced as a Christian faith leader because I know that my tradition has caused much harm and division.

Let me be very clear: any Christianity that is exclusive; any Christianity that is divisive; any Christianity that doesn't ask serious questions about structures and systems that perpetuate oppression; any Christianity that doesn't look to the person of Jesus as the ultimate authority of the tradition; any Christianity that does not lead with love, justice, mercy, and humility; any Christianity that is more judgmental than curious; any Christianity that does not take into account the fullness of who one is or asks for someone to disassociate from parts of their inherent being is not the Christianity that I profess.

Even as I am unrelentingly Christian, constantly hoping that this faith and its believers will embody Christianity in the most life-giving way possible, I am also unapologetic in my belief that God is bigger than any one religious system. This creates room in my life for multiple things to be true: (1) I believe in the God of the Christian story and form my life according to this belief, and (2) there are other, faithful ways of being and believing that also reflect the truth of who God is. It's not my place or my desire to prove anything. I am interested in faithfully honoring the relationship that I have with God and the religious belief that I profess. I respect and learn from other religious traditions and believe that God moves through anything that is steeped in love and brings to bear creativity, liberation, and sustenance for us all.

A Hard Truth

> The fact is that more people have been slaughtered in the name of religion than for any other single reason. That, that, my friends, that is true perversion![2]

The faith I profess and the religious tradition that I belong to are not perfect. What I have described here is not the form of Christianity that is often highlighted today. Throughout history, people have distorted the original goodness of Christianity. In doing so, lives have been lost, spirits have been crushed, and communities have been broken. I struggle with being connected to something that has been used to oppress and divide rather than liberate and unite.

A Christianity that seeks to conquer and disrupt is not the version of Christianity I profess or will refer to in this book.

I am committed to a version of Christianity that is steeped in love and light, in joy and compassion. It is defined by inclusivity, welcoming everyone to gather around a table that provides food for the body and for the soul. It is not a coercive faith, one that is trying to get everyone to think the same or concerned with having the right answers. It is a faith that is founded on being in right relationship, on nurturing and sustaining relationships that are life-giving.

This faith is the most important thing in my life. I am unrelentingly Christian. This means that even when Christianity fails humanity and people who claim to be Christian do and say things that are life-taking, I still fight for a faith that I *know* was given to us to bring about transformation—a faith that is concerned with reparation and restoration. I fight for a faith that invites humanity to return to itself, falling in love with God, self, and others. This love creates, liberates, and sustains us so that we can embody revolutionary relationships that have the power to heal and transform us all.

CHAPTER 2

It All Begins with Self-Love

You can't have relationships with other
people until you give birth to yourself.
—Sonia Sanchez

I'm good at relationships. In fact, if there was an Olympic event focused on relationships, I'm pretty sure I would be the contender for the gold medal.

This statement may seem ironic given that I am a thirty-seven-year-old divorcée. It's true that my romantic relationships have had varying degrees of success, and you might be wondering what makes me an expert on relationships. Well, I don't consider myself an expert. I just know that I'm damn good at relationships.

When I think about what makes a relationship successful, I simply ask myself: Did this relationship provide an opportunity for growth? For most relationships, even those that came to an end, I know without a shadow of a doubt that I experienced growth. Even relationships that may have been traumatic led, after years of healing, to redemption and growth. These relationships, whether romantic, platonic, collegial, or simply temporary, have opened my mind, heart, body, and soul to what is possible when we fully and authentically engage each other. These relationships have also shown me what can happen when we abuse one another.

Cultivating connections with people from diverse backgrounds teaches us so much about ourselves, others, and the world. When people truly connect with one another, we are given the gift of seeing the world through another's eyes, and this creates empathy. Relationships that are healthy reveal another's gifts and passions. This leads to community uplift and support.

One of my gifts is building community and curating situations that help people truly see one another. I'm talking an *Avatar*-like "I see you" experience. Feelings come pouring out, vulnerability is tentatively embraced, people practice courage (à la Brené Brown's definition of courage—showing who you are with your whole heart[1]) and are inspired to dive deeper in their relationships with themselves and with others. This is what I do. This is what I *live* for.

Being a relationship matchmaker is my calling, and I'm not simply talking about pairing people up to become romantically engaged. I carry around a mental rolodex that's constantly flipping back and forth as I meet people. Who should they know? Who might they have something in common with? What magic might be created if a new connection occurred? And voilà! A new relationship is born.

It wasn't always like this. I used to be a loner, afraid of people and of getting too close. As a child, I learned early on that people couldn't be trusted—they might leave without a moment's notice—and that people could be really mean if they didn't understand you. So I kept my distance. However, as I grew, I realized that I never wanted anyone to feel alone as long as I could prevent it. I never wanted people to be afraid of each other. I wanted people to see our shared humanity and, ultimately, the things that we had in common even as we unapologetically embraced our differences.

So like any superhero, I became what I needed for myself and decided to share this gift with the world.

The Loner

For as long as I can remember, I always felt different, as if I didn't quite belong. I never knew where this feeling came from, but a few years ago, I caught a glimpse of the girl I once was while visiting my godparents in New York. I realized that the feeling of not belonging, of not fitting in, didn't just appear. It's always been a part of who I am.

My godparents have a home video of my godbrother's birthday party at McDonald's, circa 1984. The videographer captured the sheer joy and madness of hosting a birthday party for toddlers. It was loud. Balloons floated all over the place as the adults tried to wrangle the kids to gather around a massive cake and sing an off-tempo "Happy Birthday." Ronald McDonald—that famous clown—roamed the scene, and I remember being terrified of him. He still freaks me out as a viewer some thirty years later. Children and parents were taking up every inch of the screen. I scanned the images that flashed across, wondering where I was in the midst of the chaos. The video cut to my godmother, who was standing next to my mother, both rocking early 1980s flyaway hair and big glasses that took up most of their faces. They were valiantly trying to get everyone's attention. But I was nowhere in sight.

Finally, I caught a glimpse of myself. When I found my face, I couldn't look away. There I was, sitting at a table in the midst of the party, surrounded and yet alone. Three of the four chairs at the table were empty and my three-year-old hands were clutching the bottom of the fourth. As I stared intently at this younger version of myself, I saw what I could only describe as terror. My eyes were darting around, taking in the scene. My shoulders were scrunched up, almost touching my tiny ears. I looked overwhelmed. I looked afraid. And I was all alone.

As I stared at the television, I was transported back in time. I wanted to wrap my arms around my young self and assure her that she wasn't alone. Tears sprung up and poured down my face as fear, doubt, and insecurity coursed through my body. It all made sense. The loneliness I felt, the anxiety that marked my childhood existence, the deep desire to want to belong—these were things that were with me from the very beginning. When you want to know the truth of who you are, return to the beginning of your story.

For as long as I can remember, I always wanted to fit in. I wanted to be seen and be known as the truest version of myself—even when I didn't exactly know what that version was. But I knew that I was hiding aspects of my identity. Something within us, if we pay attention, lets us know when we are embracing the fullness of who we are or when we are rejecting our truth. And even those of us who have found the truth of our identities can have a hard time fitting in—especially when our identity is one that is marginalized and ostracized.

From Loner to Friend

My family moved to Texas in 1988—one of many Black families that were a part of the New Great Migration,[2] the time between 1965 and 2000 when Blacks reversed the trend of moving from the South to the North. Our move happened during the middle of my first-grade year. To say I experienced culture shock is an understatement. I went from the concrete jungle of Queens, New York, to the suburban landscapes of Missouri City, a southwest suburb of Houston. I showed up in the laid-back South with a militant mother who was insistent that we embrace our Blackness and march to the beat of our own drummers. While I am eternally grateful for this aspect of my mother's personality, it was excruciatingly difficult for me as a child. All I wanted to do was fit in, and at every turn and in every space, I stood out.

From my hair, which was still in cornrows and beads when everyone else had a perm (the Black person's perm, which straightens our hair rather than curls it), to my clothes, which could only be described as Afrocentric when everyone else was wearing the newest styles, everything about me reeked of outsider. I spoke differently, with a New York accent rather than a Texas drawl. As if these things weren't enough, I was also an awkward child, one who was horribly uncoordinated and would rather be lost in a book than playing on the playground. These realities made for a difficult childhood, until I found my people.

Toward the end of elementary school, I became friends with a girl named Renee, who was soon to become my first BFF. Renee was the middle of three girls, and I became her fourth sister. My brother was six years younger than me, and at that time, I didn't like him all that much. Renee became my partner in crime, not that we ever got in trouble. Acing tests and being the teacher's pet were more our speed. But we did everything together. We were in the same classes and shared a lot of interests. For the first time in my life, I didn't feel so alone. Even though I still stuck out, I was sticking out *with someone else*, which made all the difference. Our social capital didn't change, but at least we had each other. We saw each other and were able to bring our *whole* selves to our relationship. And this changed everything for me.

I wouldn't have survived the first fourteen years of my life without Renee. She was my first experience with revolutionary relationships. She was the first person I can remember, from the age of seven, who loved and accepted me for who I was. I didn't have to be anyone else or do anything to earn her friendship. She shared her home and her family. I was invited on trips that created lifelong memories. I am thankful for her and for the lessons our relationship taught me.

My relationship with Renee taught me how to be a friend, but more importantly, she taught me that I was worthy of love simply because I *was*. This lesson has stayed with me. The best relationships remind us that we don't have to do anything to earn love or respect. We are accepted without question. My relationship with

Renee led me to understand that when we find our person, when we connect with people who love us unconditionally, we find belonging. This relationship left an indelible mark on how I understand friendship and was integral to my journey toward self-love.

Becoming a Relationship Connoisseur

But let there be spaces in your togetherness,
And let the winds of the heavens dance between
 you.
Love one another, but make not a bond of love:
Let it rather be a moving sea between the shores
 of your souls.[3]

No matter the quality or quantity, relationships are a fact of life. Every one of us is in relationships. Some are created by blood connections, others by experiences, and still others by choice. All of humanity is engaged in a web of relationships. Relationships form us—for better or for worse—and they have the power to change us, impacting our quality of life. Relationships can either be the glue that binds us together or the wedge that divides us, not just from each other but from ourselves.

I've always been fascinated by relationships—how they begin and how they end, how they create peace or how they create turmoil, how they liberate or how they oppress, how people choose them or how people abandon them. Relationships provide insight into who we are and how we show up in the world.

Each of us engages in and thinks about relationships in different ways. Elements of our identity, our cultural background, our economic background, our religious beliefs or lack thereof, our age and stage in life all impact our view of relationships. We don't come to understand things in a vacuum. Our whole life informs what we believe and how we think about everything!

I'm not just inquisitive about other people's relationships; I examine my own! From the exploration of my family history to the recognition that I choose to engage mainly women as my closest friends to the fact that I have quite the colorful history when it comes to my intimate connections with men, my own relationships continue to provide content for exploration, learning, and growth. Reflecting on my relationships has led me to deeper understanding of myself. I've also found that when I am at my healthiest, I'm able to reflect on my relationships and confront some hard truths about why I make certain decisions and how my actions are impacted by my relationships.

My infatuation with relationships began when I was a child. I was (and still am) an avid reader. My love of reading only intensified when I stumbled upon the world of romance novels, thanks to Renee! From Harlequin and Silhouette books to historical romance novels to thrillers that had a backdrop of a romance, I was totally and completely enamored by romance books. Authors like Terry McMillan, Julie Garwood, Pearl Cleage, Nora Roberts, Madeleine L'Engle, and Judith McNaught showed me that words have power to transport a reader into another reality.

The best stories drew me in and made me realize that I wasn't alone. I loved stories that brought people together. I loved stories that connected people from differing backgrounds. I loved when stories took me on a journey that showed how love could triumph over anything and anyone that would seek to divide.

Romance novels provided me with an alternate reality, one that invited me to imagine a world where I was loved passionately and deeply. The downside to my love affair with romance novels was that they created an unhealthy expectation for my relationships, romantic or otherwise. As I got older, I constantly sought out relationships with men that followed the arc of the relationships I read about. I was chasing passion. I wanted to feel alive, and I wanted people in my life who were exciting. I wanted to be with people who would lead me on an adventure. My expectations of people were unrealistic. This was problematic because the stories that I immersed myself in were not reality. They were a fantasy, a fairy tale that was meant to ignite fancy, not serve as a roadmap for real life.

I came to realize that the relationships I pursued were one-dimensional. They were mainly focused on what someone could do for me. They often collapsed under the weight of my unfair expectations. Truth be told, I don't think I knew or loved myself enough to be in healthy relationships. I was projecting all of my fantasies of being in love on people who simply couldn't live up to my expectations. I was chasing what I call the *love high*—the euphoric feeling that comes with being in love with a fantasy that distorts reality and hides the truth. When the high wore off, I was still longing for something I couldn't quite articulate. I was longing for something that would fill and satisfy my heart. I would then seek out the next high and the next, constantly being disappointed and wondering what was wrong with me.

It would take many more years for me to come to terms with a hard truth: in order to be in healthy relationships with others, I had to first be in a healthy relationship with myself, the first, longest, and most important relationship of my life. And this would be the most revolutionary act of all.

Relationship with Self

The most exciting, challenging, and significant relationship of them all is the one you have with yourself.[4]

Many people of Christian faith recite the greatest commandment but leave off what I consider to be the most important part! In the Christian Bible, the disciples ask Jesus what the greatest commandment is. He goes on to share not only the greatest commandment but the second commandment as well. This second commandment is often downplayed or altogether diminished.

> "Teacher, which commandment in the law is the greatest?" [Jesus] said to him, "'You shall love the Lord your God with all your heart, and with all your soul, and with all your mind.' This is the greatest and first commandment. *And a second is like it: 'You shall love your neighbor as yourself.'"*[5]

You shall love your neighbor *as yourself*. How many of us can truly say that we love or are in love with ourselves? This piece of Scripture spoken by Jesus doesn't simply command us to love our neighbors. Jesus says love your neighbor *as you love yourself*. If we don't love ourselves, how can we profess that we love our neighbor as we love ourselves? It's been a long journey for me to come to terms with the fact that I was trying to live out the greatest commandments without loving myself.

When we don't love ourselves, the relationships in our life suffer. For me, the result of not loving myself was a marriage that ended in divorce and a dearly held friendship that came to an end. While I'm clear that I wasn't the only one responsible for the end of these relationships, I have also come to realize that not loving myself or trusting my instincts leads to disastrous results.

When I met my now ex-husband, I didn't love myself. I didn't even *know* myself well enough to *like* myself. As a result, I married someone who didn't really know me because I had not taken the necessary time for reflection to know who I was at that moment in time. When we don't know ourselves (or another), it's damn near impossible to love ourselves (or another) in ways that are healthy and life-giving.

I loved my ex-husband in the best ways I knew how, but it wasn't enough because I was trying to give something that I didn't have. I was trying to be someone else, and this was inauthentic. My inability to practice grace with myself led to me not practicing grace with him. My shame about past trauma and relationships that had not been brought to light and dealt with led me to be derisive of his past. The voice in my head that reminded me day in and day out of my shortcomings became a destructive force, leading me to sabotage intimate moments. This led to a cycle that bred resentment and disconnection.

When one of my close friendships came to an end, I was devastated. It's never easy when a relationship ends, but the end of a friendship feels even more difficult than the end of a romantic relationship, because it happens far less often. Not loving myself in this context looked like not having boundaries. I found that my friend was always in need of something from me—emotional support, resources, time. Much of the time, these things were never reciprocated. I felt like I was being asked to give and give until I didn't have anything left to give, emotionally or otherwise. I was not being my authentic self. I was more worried about being alone than I was about being in a healthy relationship. And honestly, I wasn't in a healthy relationship with myself, so it was really hard to be in healthy relationships with others.

If we don't deal with the pent-up pain and trauma of our lives, with the past relationships that have ended badly, with the people and moments that have left an indelible mark on who we are and how we view the world, if we don't go back to the beginning of our story to reckon with all the shit of our lives, our present and future relationships will suffer.

The quality of our relationships with others correlates to the quality of the relationship we have with ourselves. When I survey my life, whether it's romantic relationships or friendships, I can tell when I was healthy and whole and loving myself. And to take it a step further, my relationships reach another plane when I have *fallen* in love with myself.

I recently asked a friend if he loves himself. He said, "Well, I don't hate myself." There's a big difference between not hating yourself and actually loving yourself. Many of us go through life simply tolerating ourselves. I don't want to simply tolerate myself; I want to love myself and love her deeply and passionately. I want to discover the things that make me uniquely me. I want to do things for myself that I enjoy. I want to take care of myself—mind, heart, body, and soul—so that I can live my best life. I want to practice forgiveness with myself and lavish grace upon my very being. I want to love myself, without hesitation, so I can better love others.

The difference between loving myself and being in love with myself is the difference between merely surviving and actually thriving. So many of us merely exist to survive. We don't exist to thrive. We live to get through each day, and truth be told, sometimes it's hard for us to get through each moment. We convince ourselves that we don't deserve joy or love like others do. We spend our time focused on others, and if we are honest, we do this so we don't have to focus on the shit of our own lives. We go out of our way to prove to others that we love them, but we never make the time or the effort to prove to ourselves that we deserve the same love that we try to give to others. How many of us really believe that even though we are "imperfect, and . . . wired for struggle, . . . [we] are worthy of love and belonging"?[6]

Last year my best friend and I decided to switch things up. We had spent so much time writing lists that encapsulated what we wanted in a mate. The lists have evolved as we have gotten older, moving from the superficial to the deep. Looks don't matter as much as intellect and passion do. Type of job matters less now, but a person who is excited by what they do takes its place. Rather than rewriting our lists for the hundredth time, we decided to write a list of how we hoped to be loved—what things would we want from someone that embodied their love for us. And then, we took it a step further. We challenged each other to do the things that we wrote down for ourselves rather than waiting for someone else to do it for us. The question we asked ourselves was, What would it look like to love myself the way I want to be loved by another? My answers included the following:

- Be emotionally supportive
- Be intellectually stimulating
- Be passionate
- Be affirming and be my biggest cheerleader
- Be physically connected
- Practice truth telling
- Be joyful
- Be spiritually supportive
- Engage in meaningful, quality time
- Go on an adventure

For so long, I have made loving myself someone else's job instead of taking on this holy task myself. I have devalued myself, the one made in the image of the Divine, and struggled to give myself what I need. I have forsaken the revolutionary relationship that has the power to heal every other relationship in my life—the revolutionary relationship with myself. When I don't take self-love seriously and engage it as a spiritual practice, I turn away from God's proclamation at the beginning of time that "I AM GOOD" and reject the gift of self that God has given me.

God the Lover shows us how to love ourselves—modeling self-love in the Trinitarian relationship. God invites us to be creative, to take the time to develop ideas and experiences that reflect beauty and love. God models deep rest and time away. From the Creator taking Sabbath after patiently crafting creation to Jesus spending time away from people to recharge, God models rest. I have to believe that this rest was not just about getting some sleep but about reconnecting to the source of all life in order to be reminded that it's not about what we do but simply about who we are. Practices of self-love have to slow us down and create the space for us to hear the still, small voice of God pouring love over, through, and into us.

The Trinity also shows us that when we love ourselves, we can love others better. When God takes care of Godself, the rhythms of life are restored. Jesus's ministry was strengthened precisely because he knew who he was and was clear about his purpose. The spiritual practice of self-love gets in touch with our truest self. We are renewed from within and then called to engage the world around us. Loving ourselves leads us to love others more deeply.

It's time for us to embrace self-love as a spiritual practice. We must take seriously God's proclamation that we are fearfully and wonderfully made and that we are *good*. And if we are good, we are worthy of loving ourselves. If we know better and have had enough moments that have led us to shift perspectives, then let us *do* better. This time in history is calling us to make this work our singular focus. Being devoted to loving big has to start with ourselves. In every moment, we have to commit to the practice of loving ourselves. Some days will be better than others. Some moments we might have to remind ourselves that we are worthy of deep, abiding love. But here's the thing, here's what I've learned: the more love we lavish on ourselves, the more love we have to share with others. I think this is what Jesus intended when he said to love another as we love ourselves. Jesus knew that love multiplies. It does not diminish. It always finds a way, and the more we nurture it, the more we have to give.

Revolutionary relationships cannot happen separate and apart from loving yourself.

This is why I'm the relationship connoisseur.

This is what my journey has taught me.

This is what I want for you to fully embrace.

CHAPTER 3

Rouse Your Mind

True Friendship can afford true knowledge. It does not depend on darkness and ignorance.[1]

Michael from Kenya

I met Michael when I was twenty years old, when my denomination sponsored events that invited congregations to think about global and local issues and their intersections.[2] I was invited to be a part of a group that led events around the country for congregations who wanted to expand their understanding and practices of mission, relationship, and cross-cultural competency. The leadership of the group was comprised of many young adults—artists, speakers, writers, and musicians—representing countries all over the world. This group was created and led by our mentor and role model, a woman named Sharita, who is divinity embodied. She has a way of knowing how to curate space and relationships that lead to liberation, growth, and peace.

Michael and I met through these events, but we became closer a few years later after I was tapped to research the effectiveness of short-term mission trips for the Evangelical Lutheran Church in America (ELCA). My first order of business was to gather partners from around the world who had hosted US travelers in their home countries. Michael was one of the first people I invited, and he showed up ready to share a variety of thoughts and stories. This is something that I love about Michael—he is always thinking. He is a philosopher, a sociologist, a businessman, a man of faith, and a comedian rolled into one person. He can make me think one moment and burst into laughter the next. He's awesome.

Leaders from all over Africa, Asia, the Middle East, South America, and the Caribbean were invited to join me for a multiday consultation in Chicago. My goal was to listen to their stories and ask their perspectives on Americans coming into their countries to serve. To say it was an enlightening experience is an understatement. To this day, I know that I was standing on holy ground listening to holy people share stories of frustration and anger at the ways in which people took advantage of their suffering. We created a space where people could honestly share their hurt and ask some really hard questions about intentions. I told them that while I couldn't speak for all Americans who traveled to their countries, I could listen to their stories. I could take what they shared and create best practices and training tools that groups could use so that these things wouldn't happen again.

During a particularly heated moment in our conversation, Michael began to speak, and I still remember his impassioned words to this day.

"Tell me this, Rozella. Your people spend billions of dollars on travel to our countries every year to 'help' us. They see the people. They hear the stories. They work on some projects and take some pictures. Then they go home. We are left behind, and nothing changes for us and our lives. We have heard people talk about being changed when they come back to America, but our lives go on as if nothing happened. You live in a country where your people have the power to advocate on behalf of people around the world. With the money and time spent traveling to us, why haven't laws in your country changed that impact our livelihood? Why haven't more people become politically engaged and spoken up about harmful practices and policies of the United States that negatively impact people all over the globe? If this happened, there wouldn't be a need for so-called service trips."

I was stunned and speechless. As others around the table nodded in agreement, I felt ill-equipped to respond to the rightly deserved anger that Michael was expressing. Because we were friends, I knew he wasn't mad at me, and it wasn't a personal attack. I knew that precisely because of our friendship, he felt comfortable airing his very valid frustration, and I recognized that my role was not to have all the answers or defend anyone's actions. It was simply to listen and to be present.

As others spoke up and shared their thoughts, I began to wonder if we should even do these types of trips. Were they more harmful than helpful? I asked this question, and again it was Michael who spoke up. He said, "No. Come. Bring your people. We know that getting out of one's comfort zone and experiencing another's life is necessary for transformation. But don't come to do anything. Just come and be."

This lesson has proven to be foundational for how I understand revolutionary relationships. It's never about what you *do* for another. It's always about how you *are* with another. After all, we are human *beings*, not human *doings*. Michael modeled a way of being that was not the norm for me. He challenged me to simply show up, without an agenda, and listen and learn.

For many of us, relationships are transactional. We are in relationships that help us do something, get something, or learn something. So many relationships have an agenda. Even Christianity has been guilty of encouraging people to be in relationships with others in order to get them to believe something. This way of viewing relationships has done a great disservice to our faith and our communities. Neither my faith nor my lived experiences lead me to embrace this understanding. Christianity isn't about coercion. It's about love. If I believe that God is the ultimate Lover and became human simply to show us that we were loved and model for us how to love ourselves and others, then the purpose of any relationship I'm in is to love.

By simply being who he was—by loving himself and being clear about who he was and what he was called to—Michael modeled loving me despite any shortcomings. Michael taught me that I was asleep and that there was a better way. He made me open my eyes. I will forever be indebted to him.

Awakenings

I love Jesus, who said to us:
heaven and earth will pass away.
When heaven and earth have passed away,
my word will still remain.
What was your word, Jesus?
Love? Forgiveness? Affection?
All your words were
one word: Wakeup.[3]

I really like sleeping. Actually that's an understatement. I *love* sleeping. I have an unhealthy relationship with my bed. It comforts me like no person can. Mornings are the bane of my existence. They come too quickly, and I'm rudely awakened by sunlight that doesn't care it's unwanted first thing in the morning. Anyone who knows me knows not to plan any encounter before I've had my first cup of coffee, or before 10:00 a.m.

Waking up means that it's time to move from rest to action, and I'm not always ready for this reality. It requires more energy. It requires thought. It requires that I engage the world around me.

There are two basic reactions to waking up. Some of us—myself included—hit snooze, pull the covers over our head, and go back to sleep. Others greet the day by jumping out of bed and beginning some sort of getting-ready ritual—something that helps to move them more fully toward wokeness.

I've learned a few lessons about snoozing:

- It doesn't actually provide more rest, because I'm on edge waiting for the alarm to go off again.
- It inevitably leads me to be later than I would normally be, and when I finally do get out of bed, I find myself rushed and out of breath.

So, snoozing actually keeps me from fully waking up and greeting the day with an open heart and an open mind. When I focus more on what I'm leaving behind than what could be, I not only limit myself but also miss out on the people and lessons life is waiting to share with me.

This is not only true of waking up from sleep. It is also true of waking up to the realities of life that are often ignored. Too many of us choose to stay in places that are comfortable but isolating. Too many of us choose situations that are known to us but that no longer serve our growth.

There's something to be said for waking up, for the moments in our life when we realize we have been asleep. Waking up can be a jarring experience. Think of the loud, clanging alarm clock that goes off while you are in dreamland. You come to with a jolt that rocks you and leaves your heart racing. It can be a struggle to get your bearings. You search around for something or someone that grounds you. You take several deep breaths in order to come back to center. And we all have a choice, either to hit the snooze button or to wake up.

Ignorance Is Not Bliss

Where justice is denied, where poverty is enforced, where ignorance prevails, and where any one class is made to feel that society is an organized conspiracy to oppress, rob and degrade them, neither persons nor property will be safe.[4]

Meeting Michael and maintaining a relationship with him taught me how to think differently. I started to ask questions about how society was ordered. I began to ask questions about how resources are distributed and why some populations experience life very differently than other populations. I came to see how disconnected we truly are. We don't know what's happening with our neighbors, we don't know what's happening with our family members—we don't know what's happening with people in our country let alone with people in our community. So many of us living in the United States are ignorant of the things that happen outside of our immediate vicinity. The saying "out of sight, out of mind" applies to so many of us when it comes to the reality of those we don't know.

My relationship with Michael led me to realize that knowing is necessary if change is to happen. Michael taught me a very important lesson. In order for things to change, you have to be willing to use all of your senses to connect to another. And once you do this, it becomes impossible, if not inhumane, to ignore the suffering you've witnessed. Once you see, you can't unsee. Once you know, you can't unknow. Once you feel, you can't unfeel.

Michael taught me that ignorance is a privilege that can be destructive. The very fact that I, a citizen of the United States, can go a week not hearing or seeing anything other than what I want to hear or see is problematic. The bubbles that we live in keep us separate from one another. This leads to an isolation so deep that we don't even recognize how disconnected we truly are.

Michael introduced me to a more authentic and present way of being. My relationship with him has led me to travel more, and in those travels, I prioritize presence and relationship over constant work. I have traveled throughout Europe, Africa, the Middle East, Asia, and Latin America. While all of the places and people I visit teach me more about the power of relationships, the Middle East holds a special place in my heart.

I began traveling to the Middle East in 2013. I participated in a trip led by dear friends who invited young adults from the DC area to travel to Israel and Palestine for a couple of weeks. The purpose of this trip was to learn about the people and the place, with special attention paid to the military occupation of the Palestinian people and their land. We went as partners of the Lutheran church in the region, and a key piece of this partnership was to accompany our fellow humans who live there. We didn't go to build anything, start a project, or give money. We went simply to listen and learn. Much of our learning happened around tables with tea in people's homes. We were forced to slow down and listen to holy stories of survival, of living, and of loving. In that context, there is nothing that I can do to change the reality. When I am in the Middle East, I practice presence every minute of every day, and this is a gift I take with me when I leave that holy land.

I continue to travel to the region, including to Egypt, Jordan, the United Arab Emirates, and Israel and Palestine. I go to continue deepening relationships and to let my friends know that my relationship with them is not dependent on what they do. I love them for who they are, and because I love them and myself, I have no choice but to live a life that reflects their values and my values.

I was implicitly taught that relationships were about what I did for another person. I am a woman, a Black woman, so I know that the socialization I received in every space—the home, the world, my church—led me to believe that I was meant to constantly give and never expect anything in return. This thinking is damaging so many people today. Our relationships should reflect the Divine Lover and be life-giving, risk-taking, vulnerable, forgiving, gracious, diverse, and hold us accountable. Our relationships become revolutionary when they mirror the Lover and lead us to create, liberate, and sustain ourselves and each other.

I am convinced that the things I say I value in my context in the United States are intimately bound up with and inextricably linked to the reality of my global partners. I am made better, I see more clearly, and I fight more passionately for the issues in my local community based on the things I learn from the global community.

I recognize that not everyone has the means to travel and engage with folks around the world. The beauty of this time in history is that we have technology that gives us access to different communities and their stories. You don't have to travel far if you live in the United States to encounter someone who is different from you. And that's the biggest lesson of all—seeing what was previously invisible because I took the blinders off and was open to the multiple realties that exist around me on a daily basis. Until we recognize this truth and come together with a unified voice to combat the evils that oppress us all, we will continue to be in bondage. Until all are free, none are free.

When I talk about freedom, I'm not referring to the typical US definition of freedom: being free to do and say what one wants and not being ruled by anyone. My understanding of freedom flows from my faith. Because of who God is and how God showed up in Jesus, I have been redeemed. I am no longer subject to the ways of this world. I am free to live a life modeled after Christ, a life focused on love of self, others, and God. This freedom releases me from worrying about what will happen after this life ends and beckons me to focus on the reality of life today. I am called out to be in relationship and address the systems and structures that lead us to bondage of any kind. And I recognize that if any member of the human family experiences oppression or stigma, shame or disease, I too experience it because our lives are bound. That's what my faith and my relationship with Michael have taught me. In the words of Dr. Martin Luther King Jr.,

> I am cognizant of the interrelatedness of all communities and states. . . . We are caught in an inescapable network of mutuality, tied in a single garment of destiny. Whatever affects one directly, affects all indirectly.[5]

Freedom begins with waking up, with rousing our minds from sleep that threatens to keep us in bondage. We can only be free when we come to recognize that our liberation is bound, and we only come to understand this when we wake up. Revolutionary relationships lead to this type of awakening.

Revolutionary relationships help us understand that our lives are fractured. They reflect back to us what we choose not to see or what we don't even realize exists. I've learned that healing first begins with acknowledging that something is broken or diseased. If we are not in relationship with people who help us identify the issue, we can't move toward healing.

I am forever indebted to Michael and his perspectives. Our relationship led me to view the world and others through a new lens. My mind has been awakened, and I will never be the same. I live with an understanding of a new world order.

A New World Order

If you have come here to help me, you are wasting your time.

But if you have come because your liberation is bound up with mine, then let us work together.[6]

My faith has forever been impacted by my relationship with Michael. From a theological perspective, I consistently ask questions of what's being said, taught, or implied. I want to know how what's being shared reflects God as Lover. If a perspective isn't creative, liberating, and sustaining, I know it is not reflective of the God who orders my life. And what I've found is that so many communities, leaders, and popular theological perspectives *don't* reflect this God. It's increasingly hard to find community because of this orientation and lens. I am no longer willing to participate in communities that, for example, only use male language to describe God or belittle the voices of women. Communities that don't focus on discipleship steeped in relationship are ruled out. Places where the gospel of Jesus Christ isn't front and center, with a clear connection to social justice, are disappointing.

While my faith tradition taught me so much about a God who is creative, liberating, and sustaining, it did not fully prepare me for the change in my life that would come with falling in love with Jesus and with myself. Because of our emphasis on God's grace and God's faithfulness over and above our ability to earn our salvation, my tradition tends to shy away from a focus on actions in the world. While I absolutely rely on God's grace, I believe that something has been lost because we don't talk about how our faith changes our lives in concrete ways that are reflected in the way we order our lives. My relationship with Michael brings this to the forefront. Our emphasis on grace has led to a lackluster commitment to exploring the connections between faith and action. We barely focus on discipleship, and this has led to stagnant communities of faith.

On the other hand, I also challenge a self-sacrificing model that says that my faith should lead me to totally deny myself at all costs. This way of being has been destructive, particularly for women of color and others on the margins. In a perverse way, a theological focus on sacrifice has led many to deny themselves health and wellness in order to appease a seemingly unappeasable God. I will not deny the very essence and being that

God created in the Divine image. In fact, I will claim it, unapologetically, and cultivate it through practices that lead me to more deeply love God and myself. I don't believe that God calls us to sacrifice in ways that are life-taking. I believe God calls us to sacrifice anything that would stand in the way of allowing us to receive God's love for us, anything that stands in the way of us loving ourselves and loving other.

My relationship with Michael has led me to question my understandings of faith, self-love, and relationships. This has led to a new way of being and has caused me to commit to embodying my values and beliefs in new ways. My life has forever been changed. This has caused some grief and heartache in my life because I have had to let go of long-standing beliefs and relation-ships that no longer serve me well. I now see the world through a different lens, and my life has fundamentally been altered.

CHAPTER 4

Repair Your Heart

*I was still mourning—clinging to the broken heart
of girlhood, to broken connections. When that
mourning ceased I was able to love again.*
—bell hooks[1]

Brokenhearted Girl

My heart was broken at a young age, and I'm not talk-ing about romantic heartbreak. I'm referring to the heartbreaks of life, to the things that bring about deep disappointment and can instill a sense of unworthiness within. We often think of heartbreak strictly in roman-tic terms, but I think heartbreak includes anything that disappoints us, traumatizes us, or alters our identity in such a way that we forget our beloved nature. Heart-break makes us think we need to work for our goodness instead of simply accepting it.

My heart wasn't broken purposely or maliciously, but that's the thing about heartbreak—it doesn't have to be intentional in order to be devastating. Heartbreak happens at an interpersonal level when the people we are closest to mishandle or abuse our trust. Heartbreak happens on a larger scale when we witness and experience widespread oppression, disconnection, and pain. Heartbreak is a fact of life. If you are living, your heart will be broken at some point.

As I came of age, I don't think I realized that I was living with a broken heart. The deep ache I experienced became normal. Instead of living like I was a beloved child of God, I lived as though I was lacking—as if my personhood was fundamentally unworthy. I engaged in maladaptive ways of being and thinking because that was what I knew. When we don't believe we are worthy of love, we seek out anything and everything to fill the void. I tried to fill the void by overachieving as a student, always wanting to be the best and to receive affirmations that never provided the relief that I sought. I entered romantic relationships with people who didn't have the capacity to love me in the ways that I needed them to. My broken heart was seeking restoration by any means necessary, and that often led to more pain. It's only in retrospect that I began to understand how my life was formed around that which broke me rather than that which gave me life.

The two people who hurt me most were the two men who were supposed to love me best: the two father figures in my life. Some of the most painful experiences of my life came from people who loved me deeply but who didn't have the capacity to be present in ways that I needed. The first man to break my heart was my biological father.

I am the youngest of my biological father's four children by three different women. My father was addicted to drugs and alcohol when I was conceived. Even though he and my mother had been dating for a while, my mother drew a line in the sand after I was born. She didn't want to raise a child with an addict, so she left my father. I wasn't even a year old when this happened. Looking back, the only memories I have of my dad were random weekends at his mom's house when my siblings and I would be dropped off. One of the most vivid memories of my childhood was my father's love of beer. He always had a beer in his hand, even when he was driving.

This all changed when my mother met my stepfather and we moved to Texas when I was six. After that, I only remember a few phone calls from my dad, the occasional birthday card, and a couple of trips to see him during summer break. I never stayed with him and would only see him in passing or for a day or two.

Years later I remember angrily accusing my dad of not fighting hard enough for me, of letting me go without considering the impact this would have on me. While my feelings were valid, I came to realize that I lived with only one side of a very complicated story. There was more to the situation that I didn't know, but the thing that stuck with me was that the man who was supposed to love me first chose not to be present. This created in me a deep desire to be fought for, to be fully seen and loved by men who would choose me. And this led me to question if I was enough, in every area of my life, for years to come.

The second man to break my heart was my step-father. He and my mother met when I was three and married when I was five. They gave birth to my younger brother, and we all relocated from New York to Texas. I called him dad, and he treated me like his daughter. He wasn't very emotive, and I honestly don't remember him ever saying he loved me, but I knew he cared. He provided for our family, acting as a stay-at-home dad because he was considerably older than my mother and had retired before we moved to Texas. I thought we were pretty close and our family made a great team.

My life changed when my mother and my stepfather announced that they were getting a divorce when I was twelve. The world as I knew it tilted on its axis. For the first time in my life, I realized that I was a stepchild, that I wasn't really a part of this family that I thought existed, and that my stepfather wasn't really my father. After the divorce, I was not a part of the visitation agreement that allowed my brother to go to his dad's house on alternating weekends. My brother would leave, and I would stay back with my mother. My stepfather went from being my primary caregiver to being someone I saw only when we dropped off or picked up my brother. Once again, a man who was supposed to love and care for me left and didn't choose me. I was left reeling. How did a parent just disappear from a child's life? What was wrong with me that made it so easy for the men in my life to walk away? What did I do or say that made me unlovable and undesirable? Where does the love go?

These questions took root in my head and in my heart and before I even realized it, I was living a brokenhearted life.

A Brokenhearted Existence

There are two main responses to living a brokenhearted existence. Some harden their exterior so that nothing penetrates their heart. Their past constantly informs their present, and they make decisions that tend to be focused on protecting what's left versus opening up to what could be. They are not interested in vulnerability for vulnerability's sake. Their goal is to survive and to do so in ways that block out anything and everything that might cause them additional pain. So much of their life is focused on maintaining a wall that keeps others out. Even as they crave connection, they don't want to get too close to others because that has the potential to take them back to what broke their heart.

Others—like me—try to mend a broken heart by chasing that which broke it in the first place. Instead of hardening, we soften and bend and lose our identity. We continue to find ourselves in spaces and with people who hurt us rather than contribute to our healing. We throw all caution to the wind and think boundaries are unnecessary. Our deepest desire is to be loved and to be seen, so we go to extraordinary lengths to make this a reality. Being loved, accepted, and seen as worthy become our focus, and instead of seeking healing to address the brokenness within, we are constantly looking to external sources to fix us.

It doesn't matter if you are a brokenhearted person living with a hardened exterior or if you are living with no discernible boundaries. When you live life from your brokenness and haven't sought healing, you're not really living. You're simply existing. And I don't believe that our Creator desires for us to merely survive. We were created to *thrive*. When we don't deal with our brokenness, every other part of our life is impacted. Our relationships, our work, our view of self all suffer when we don't attend to that which ails us. And neither approach—pushing people away or looking to others to heal us—will work.

I went from being the brokenhearted girl living a brokenhearted existence to a woman on fire. And this wasn't a good thing. I burned everything down around me—including myself and my relationships.

Woman on Fire

I used to envision my heart as a busted organ with Band-Aids keeping it together as it limped along. It had holes and blocked arteries. It couldn't really pump blood to the other organs in my body because it was weak. It barely beat, and struggled to sustain my life. This tattered heart was first broken by my fathers and continued to be broken by the men I chose to engage in intimate relationships. My tattered heart impacted how I viewed myself and the quality of my relationships across the board.

After my mother and my stepfather divorced, my biological parents reconciled and married each other. In the span of two years, my family drastically changed. I began high school living with the father I didn't know while the father who raised me disappeared. To say that I was confused is an understatement. I had no idea how to feel or what it all meant. I just remember being sad and angry and misunderstood.

So like any human being, I looked for an outlet, for some relief from the emotional roller coaster that was my life. Seeking attention from men served as a distraction and became my focus. I loved falling in love, and I loved being in a relationship. I dated all different types of guys throughout high school. I would chase them until they fell in love with me (or whatever the equivalent of this is as a teenager) and then I would lose interest. This was my pattern: choose a guy, chase a guy, catch a guy, create a super-intricate fantasy that involved us staying together forever and ever, and then promptly lose interest and cut him loose.

This way of being continued in college and became more dangerous when sex was involved. I wasn't just playing games in my head and heart, I was playing games with my body, and this left a mark on my spirit. Suddenly, the fantasies I created had repercussions. Every time I gave my body away, I lost a piece of my already-fractured existence. Trying to love with your body when you are not comfortable in your skin or even aware of the significance of the acts can be dangerous.

My freshman year at Spelman College, the women on my floor in the dorm created superlatives. I was given two honors: Most Likely to Marry a Morehouse Man and Most Missing-in-Action Roommate. These two went hand-in-hand. I was the most missing-in-action roommate because I was *always* at Morehouse College.

Even in the face of failure, I didn't necessarily change how I engaged men. I just tried harder. I doubled down on my efforts and chased the hell out of them. I became determined to get them to fall in love with me at all costs. This way of being culminated in a marriage to a man I loved but who I wasn't in love with. I didn't love myself, and it became impossible to give something to him that I didn't give to myself.

I married my ex-husband around the same time I began seminary. I didn't know it at the time, but in seminary I would find the very thing I was looking for in the most unexpected place. For my entire life I had been looking for validation through other people. Suddenly, I was confronted with the truth that the healing I sought could only be found in God, in a revolutionary relationship with a God who created me and knew my inmost parts. I was looking for something external to myself, without realizing it already existed within me. This time in my life, which included a marriage, the start of theological studies, and therapy, opened my eyes and heart to a feminine God that would begin the process of healing that I so desperately longed for.

I Met God and She's Female

i found god in myself
& i loved her / i loved her fiercely[2]

My journey toward healing happened while I was engaging a process of unbecoming. I was in a marriage that I regretted from the moment I said yes. I was living in a depressing city, beginning a journey toward professional church leadership that included graduate work. I had not dealt with my past or any feelings that I kept tightly locked within. It is said that depression is anger turned inward, so it's no surprise that I also dealt with major depression and anxiety during this time.

Here's what I've learned about healing: it always gets worse before it gets better. Healing requires a cleaning out of the wounds of our life. And this is painful. It's messy. It can lead us to think, again and again, that we just want to go back to the way things were. We know how to survive in the brokenness. But I no longer wanted to simply survive. I wanted to thrive. When we get a glimpse of how life can be, of the joy and fullness and passion that's a part of a life that has been restored to wholeness, it's hard to go back to the way things were. I had a sense that the life I was living was not the life that God desired for me. Everything came to a head during this season.

Seminary in and of itself is a time of deconstruction. It's designed to flip your thinking upside down and inside out. Everything I thought I knew about my religious tradition I suddenly had to examine and question. The faith that I professed before I entered seminary is not the faith I profess today. My faith has deepened and expanded. The more I discover about God, the more I question. I appreciated this type of inquiry because it took my mind off the life that I was living and the person I had become. I was exposed to new ways of thinking about God. I encountered people from diverse backgrounds, some of whom were not from the Christian tradition. This was a time of growth, of reimagining who God is and how my faith could be expanded.

I was introduced to Womanist theology during this time, and it forever changed how I think about God, myself, and my relationships. Womanist theology was first defined by Alice Walker in her book *In Search of Our Mothers' Gardens*. Womanist theologians focus on the lived reality of Black women and their relationship with God. Womanist theology validated that my lived experience as a Black woman was seen, heard, and known by God. Taking it a step further, it challenged any notion that the suffering I had experienced was caused by God or was necessary for redemption.

This has huge implications for what it means to be made in the image of God. If I, a Black woman who experiences oppression and heartbreak, was made in the image of God, then God is a Black woman who experiences oppression and heartbreak. Instead of desperately trying to be seen and known by the men in my life or to be validated because of my accomplishments, I recognized that I was already seen and known by the God of my life. And she loves me fiercely.

Encountering this perspective was like encountering the part of myself that I had been longing for, the self that I couldn't fully articulate yet was exactly who I was created to be. God was constantly inviting me to shift my perspective of my story, of my heartbreak, and of the relationships in my life. I began the journey of rewriting my story and experiencing reparation—the repairing of my heart. This reparation involved the work of falling in love with myself—of recognizing and believing that I was made in the image of God—and going back to the beginning, to the first heartbreak, to find healing.

Daddy's Girl

Unconditional love. Respect. Affirmation. To be truly seen and known and loved despite your flaws. These are the things that all of us want and need. In a perfect world, our parents provide these things for us when we are young. But we don't live in a perfect world. Our parents are human and they fall short. Most of them do the best they can with what they were given. In my case, not having a father figure who was able to model and provide these things for me at a young age led me to a broken heart.

The relationship that I have with my biological father today is radically changed. Today, I am undeniably and unapologetically a daddy's girl. Over the last twenty years, my father and I have grown into a connection that's everything I ever wanted or could have hoped for. We have both evolved, choosing to listen to each other and recognize the fullness of who we are—our flaws, our hopes, our disappointments, and our struggles. My perspectives have shifted, and I've grown curious about my dad's life rather than judgmental. When we reach adulthood, we have an opportunity to get to know our parents as human beings, and knowing my dad in this way has been such a gift.

It's taken time and hard work for us to get here. In order for something to be healed, we have to recognize that it's broken. And we have to do the work of excavation in order to find the root cause of the brokenness. The root cause of my heartbreak was being disconnected from my dad and believing the worst about him and myself. I believed he didn't want me, and I believed that I was unlovable. Neither of these beliefs were true, but they were so deeply engrained in my psyche that I had to name them and root them out in order to find healing.

One of my favorite types of art forms is Kintsukuroi, which comes from the Japanese tradition. This is the practice of repairing broken pottery with lacquer resin laced with gold. Instead of trying to hide the brokenness of the pottery, the gold highlights where the pottery was broken, creating a new interpretation of an old object.

The broken pieces are highlighted rather than hidden, or worse, discarded.

My relationship with my dad has been mended. The broken pieces are still there, but the cracks in my heart are now filled in with God's grace and love for the two of us. My heart is stronger as I've sought to repair this relationship, which couldn't happen until I came to terms with the brokenness within. My dad and I have a revolutionary relationship, and it has proven to have the power to bring about healing.

In order to experience healing, you first have to recognize what is broken. You have to be honest with yourself and examine your life. Repairing your heart is not for the timid. It requires reflection, patience, and grace. There have been many times in my life that I wanted to return to old ways of being—to the self that I had grown accustomed to. But this was not what my heart needed. In order to experience healing, I had to do the hard work of seeking out a God who knows and sees me, a God who loves me unconditionally. In doing this, I began the process of falling in love with myself and then was able to recognize that everything I had been seeking was already present. I found healing when I was able to embrace forgiveness. God mended a foundational relationship that has affirmed my Divine identity and reminded me, day in and day out, of my inherent worth.

CHAPTER 5

Reform Your Body

apologize to your body.
maybe,
that's where the healing begins.
—Nayyirah Waheed[1]

Bootylicious

I have a complicated relationship with my body. Many of my friends would tell you that I am extremely comfortable in my skin. Some might say that I'm *too* comfortable. Most of my close friends and family have seen me naked. I enjoy being naked. I have no issues with bodily functions. I find joy in my body and marvel at her versatility. I feel most grounded when I am fully in my body—when I'm dancing, when I'm using my hands to create art, when I'm having sex, when I'm laughing so hard that my belly aches. When I am in my body, my mind stops racing and time stands still. I am able to be present in ways that put me in touch with my deepest feelings and heartfelt desires.

There are days when I love my body so much. I look at my naked form in the mirror and examine her from every angle. I love my skin, which is the color of caramel and tans easily. In the summer, the red undertones of my Puerto Rican heritage are revealed. In the winter, my skin lightens up, and I nourish it to keep it supple and soft. I love my newfound breasts—a product of weight gain. When I was young, I was a slender, athletic girl. The only complaint that I had about my body was that I was a part of the itty-bitty titty committee. I sprouted early and started wearing a bra in the fourth grade. My bra size did not change from the time I was ten until I was twenty-one, holding steady at 34A. I often wished for larger breasts, and now, I have them!

I love the fullness of my body that has emerged as I've gotten older—the roundness of my hips and butt. There is no denying that I am a grown woman. On the days when I'm feeling love for my body, I speak life over her, praising my body for all she's been through—for healing from traumatic experiences, for recovering from disease and illness, for being the form that God gifted me with.

But, as I said, my relationship with my body is complicated. Some days, I look at this same body and I say and think things about her that I would never say or think about anyone else. I look at myself with disgust. I hate the weight that I've gained. I lament that my knees crack when I stand up too quickly and that my back aches after a long day on my feet. I've undergone surgery and struggled with the limits placed on my body as I healed. During these times, my inner dialogue reveals a level of self-loathing for my body and her changing capacity.

I experience what can only be described as a sort of cognitive dissonance when it comes to dealing with my body. I have inconsistent thoughts about her that I know are a result of childhood trauma, family dynamics, and societal views and expectations of what it means to be a woman and live in a female body.

Disconnection

At an early age, I learned that the body I inhabited was not my own—that others could do what they wanted to it and that I had little control over how it was treated. I experienced sexual trauma as a child. It would take almost twenty-five years for me to confront the impact of these experiences and how it affected my relationships. I was also raised by parents who used spanking as a means of punishment—a practice I now condemn. I remember feeling so much anger when I was spanked, even though it didn't occur frequently. I didn't understand how the same parents who taught me not to use physical violence could turn around and use violence against me. I remember feeling powerless in these moments, much like I did when I experienced sexual trauma. These two acts had one thing in common: they taught me that my body was not my own. Anyone who had more power over me could use that power at any time, and I was helpless to stop them.

When I became sexually active at sixteen, I began to experience my body differently. All of a sudden, I was able to choose who had access to my body. I realized the power my body had, what some might term the "power of the pussy." Around this same time, my parents split up and I learned what it felt like to have my heart broken by the men in my life. I believed that the healing I was seeking could be found in sex. However, this was immature sex engaged in by an immature girl, one who didn't know herself, her body, or the deeper consequences of giving others access to her body.

Don't get me wrong. I don't believe that sex is bad. It is a gift created by God that has incredible power, and I thank God for the gift of sex regularly. I have learned how to honor its power, and I now engage it as a mature adult who enjoys it very much. However, like anything that is powerful, if misused or abused, sex can have dire consequences.

When I got to college, I lost my damn mind. I was away from home for the first time in a place that promoted liberation and freedom among women. But here's the thing about freedom (especially when you have not been prepared for it): when all doors are open to us, that includes doors that lead to harm. Freedom must be respected or else it can destroy a person. As a freshman in college, I didn't understand the power that I carried in my body and how sex could lead to the destruction of my identity and my relationships when abused.

During this time, I vacillated between enjoying sexual acts and feeling deep shame. I was on an emotional roller coaster, trying to heal past wounds by engaging in relationships with a variety of men but only finding myself retraumatized. After every failed relationship or encounter, I would spiral deeper into depression, wondering what was wrong with me and how I should behave differently in the future. Such intense emotions coursed through me that at some point, I decided to vote my feelings off the island and simply engage in sex without an emotional connection because that's what I thought men wanted—and I wanted to be wanted by men. I didn't care anymore about how I felt or about my pleasure or even about the consequences. The power that I thought I was exhibiting by choosing to be sexually active became the shackles that kept me in a cycle of self-loathing, depression, and confusion.

Here's the thing: no matter how hard we try, we cannot separate our emotions from our bodies. I tried this for a very long time and what I learned was that my emotions would find a way to come out regardless of how I tried to hide or suppress them. Each new experience and person became another layer that my body needed to carry, so that soon I was carrying around the things that had been done to me, the things that I allowed to be done to me, and other people's baggage—their hurt and pain, how they viewed me, their insecurities—because I allowed them into my body.

This came to a head when I got married. There's nothing like marriage to reveal your flaws, your struggles, and all the things that you haven't dealt with emotionally. While the details of my marriage and subsequent divorce are complex, I now see the glaring truth that I was a woman who was disconnected from her body and could not engage in sex intimately with my husband. I was twenty-seven before I confronted the trauma of my life. Or maybe I should say, I was twenty-seven when the trauma of my life confronted me.

Be Sexy. Sexy Is Bad

I was a cheerleader in middle school and high school. I loved cheering, especially lifting people up and getting the crowd excited. I also loved the uniforms and the attention that came with being in front of crowds. My cheerleading squad fundraised for our competitions. We held traditional fundraisers like candy sales and car washes, but our most successful fundraiser included my squad mates and me wearing short shorts, crop tops, and fake pony-tails. We donned this uniform and chose a busy street corner in our hometown. We created signs and stood on the corner with buckets. It's amazing how much money twelve scantily clad teenage girls can raise in a few hours.

Looking back, I learned a lesson that I carry with me even today. My body is a commodity, and people are willing to pay a high price for it as long as it looks a certain way. At sixteen, I knew that I could get things I wanted from people, especially from men, if I dressed a certain way and smiled just right. However, I also received the message that spending too much time on my looks or being provocatively dressed in other situations would lead people to think negatively of me or would give them the impression that they could use and abuse my body. My squad mates and I received lectures about how to carry ourselves and what we could and couldn't wear as representatives of my high school. Women are constantly given competing messages about who we should be and how we should look. Be sexy, but sexy is bad. Take care of your body, but don't obsess over your body. You're fine just the way you are, but you could look better. Be financially responsible, but buy things to make yourself look better, smell better, and feel better. Your body is a commodity, but no one wants a woman who sells herself.

I see these messages continue to play out in our society today, and it affects us all. I recently spent time with my eleven-year-old niece. She's an artist and writer and was looking for a new journal. I had a few extra ones at home, some made by a feminist artist who paints journal covers with different sayings. My niece asked me about them, and I told her she could choose one to take home. She chose the one with the saying: "Consent is mandatory and sexy." I explained to her what it meant, and we went about our merry way.

Later that evening, my niece was using her journal and my brother—her father—saw the cover. He took the journal from her and began vigorously scratching out the word *sexy*. I watched, incredulous, as he freaked out about the word.

"Roze, you can't give her things like this! She doesn't need to know what sexy is."

"Why not?" I responded. "There's nothing wrong with the word, and how will she know unless we teach her?!"

My brother turned to his daughter and said, "You don't need to be sexy."

We got into a heated debate. Mind you, my brother *loves* sexy women, but in that moment he had no tolerance for the idea that his daughter might think about sex or be sexy one day.

This is how it begins. We are taught dueling messages about our bodies, and these messages impact how we relate to ourselves and to each other. We treat our bodies as objects, as things disconnected from our minds and hearts. We don't treat our bodies as living, breathing organisms that need to be nurtured, affirmed, and healed. When we are not comfortable in our skin, when we don't embrace the physical aspect of our identity, it becomes hard for us to embrace and respect another's physical identity. Being in revolutionary relationship with yourself and with others means that you come to terms with the physicality of humanity. We were not made as formless beings. We were created with a body, in the image of God. And when God created us, we were called good, holy, and whole.

The *Imago Dei*

Christians believe that all people are created in the image of God—the *imago Dei*. This concept is not simply a theory to me. It's something that I believe to be true. Humankind is made in the likeness of God—mind, heart, body, and soul. We are not God, but our form has been patterned after God. Taking it a step further, I believe that my body is also formed in the likeness of God, as is yours. Each body reflects an aspect of the

Divine, with our diverse skin tones, abilities, identities, shapes, and sizes. We get a glimpse of how creative our God is when we consider that all of humanity is made in God's Divine image. It's not just that God is creative enough to create diversity. God is diversity. God's nature embodies the very creation that God saw fit to breathe into being.

Not only are we made in the image of God, but God also names creation as fundamentally good. This means that the body is good! The functions of the body are not bad. However, because we are broken, we do things to ourselves and to others that distort the original goodness of what God has created—perpetuating trauma, misusing and abusing physical power over another, dehumanizing other human beings, commodifying our physical forms for pleasure without regard to the emotional and mental consequences of this commodification, and anything else that leads us to devalue and abuse our physical forms.

When we think about God in the Trinity, or God as Lover, we see that the physical body matters. It matters so much that the God without a form chose to take on a form and live alongside humanity. As a Christian, my faith begins with the incarnation. In Jesus, I believe that the body is given another stamp of approval. God chose to be born of a woman, coming into being like every other human and moving through childhood to adulthood. In Jesus, we see God as a physical being, living, loving, learning, and ultimately liberating. Jesus liberated old ways of being and believing so that new ways of living and loving could be experienced. This liberation happened through a body. I believe that when we focus on healing our physical bodies, we experience liberation.

Too often, Christians have glamorized the death of God in ways that lead us to turn a blind eye toward the physical suffering of those in our midst. Looking at Jesus as an example, we wrongly believe that suffering either has a purpose or will be redeemed at a later point in time. What if we believed that God came to live and not to die? What if we believed that the ultimate beauty of the Christian story was in the mysterious, miraculous, and mystical incarnation? This would drastically change how those of us called Christ followers show up in the world, how we treat our bodies and other people's bodies.

By starting with the premise that God came to live rather than to die and embracing the fact that Jesus took on flesh and this act brought about liberation, we can begin to understand the power of embracing our bodies. As I dealt with my past trauma and became reacquainted with my body, I experienced healing and liberation. I reconnected my body to my mind, heart, and soul. I forgave myself for how I treated my body.

I started to take better care of my body and found joy within her. I embraced a newfound love of sex and intimacy, one that respected who I was, what I desired, and how I wanted to be treated. When I believed that I was truly made in the image of God, I treated myself differently. And it led me to another revelation: the more healing and liberation I experienced personally, the more healing and liberation I wanted others to experience too.

My Body Matters

When I'm asked to speak at events, I often ask groups—largely comprised of white people—what they see when they look at me. These are people who respect me and have shown up to hear me speak because of who I am. People respond with all sorts of answers: they see a smart woman, a confident woman, a stylish woman, an articulate woman, and the list goes on and on.

Finally, after the hundredth response, I emphatically ask, "What do you SEE when you look at me?"

Every now and then, a brave, trembling voice will say, "You're Black?"

To which I reply, "YES! I am Black!"

I do this to prove a point. We have been conditioned that seeing a person's skin color or any other physical characteristic is somehow politically incorrect. I need people to see my skin color—to start to pay attention to their thoughts when they notice my Blackness, to understand that the person I am can't be separated from my Blackness, that my Blackness means something in the world today.

As a Black woman growing up in the United States, I was told that my body doesn't matter, that it isn't seen as valuable. I never saw images in popular culture that reflected my identity, leading me to wonder if there was something wrong with my image. As a Black woman, I live at the intersection of two marginalized communities. It's been a fight to love all of me—my Blackness and my femaleness—because both aspects of who I am have been historically and repeatedly dehumanized.

My body is the descendant of slaves who were brought to the Caribbean and the United States from West Africa. I am part of a lineage of bodies that were bought and sold as property. I am the offspring of those who survived the Middle Passage, of those who lived through generations of chattel slavery, Reconstruction, Jim Crow, the Civil Rights Movement, and now the Movement for Black Lives. My body matters because the rights afforded to me, the spaces that I can and cannot inhabit, the people I can or cannot be in relationship with, the jobs I can or cannot hold are all based on my *body*. My body matters because the society I live in was built by the work, backs, and blood of my ancestors—all of which have physical implications. My body matters not because it's better than anyone else's body but precisely because it's been abused and dehumanized. I was not created to be property and to be mistreated. I was created in the image of God, so when my body is rendered invaluable, God is too.

My life has been changed by the ongoing deaths of Black and brown bodies. When Trayvon Martin was killed in 2012, I began to pay more attention to public discourse about race, rights, and relationships in a new way. With each death of a Black or brown person, it became clear that our lives were seen as less than those of our white counterparts. As a woman, I also noticed how the media uplifted the deaths of Black and brown men more than they did the deaths of women. When Sandra Bland died, I recognized how respectability politics was used to define what "type" of woman she was.

"If she would have just kept her mouth shut . . ." as if keeping quiet has ever been the determining factor for whether or not a Black person was treated respectfully.

Whether it was the death of a Black person at the hands of a white police officer or some other circumstance, the ways that we were portrayed continually showed that our bodies didn't matter. Black and brown people and transgender women of color were all portrayed as the ones responsible for their own deaths. The rallying cry of Black Lives Matter made complete sense to me. People of a darker hue are not afforded the same rights and respect as white people. Black Lives Matter isn't about erasing the humanity of others; it's about reclaiming the humanity of us all.

The incarnation also shows me that if I'm made in the image of God, I am also an embodiment of the Divine. Me with my vagina. Me with my Black skin. In the fullness of who I am, I represent and reflect the Divine. We are able to dehumanize another when we don't fully embrace our own humanity or recognize one another as embodiments of God's very self. Revolutionary relationships bring us back to ourselves and each other, honoring our bodies and reforming how we treat ourselves and others. As long as we treat each other differently and negatively based on physical characteristics, we are not honoring our body or the body of the Divine. We will not experience healing until we apologize to our own bodies and others' bodies. We will not experience liberation until we put our bodies in the places and spaces that reflect our values.

CHAPTER 6

Restore Your Soul

Janie . . . felt a soul-crushing love. So her soul
crawled out from its hiding place.
—Zora Neale Hurston[1]

Hide and Seek

"How is it with your soul?"

As this question left the lips of my spiritual director, I felt time stop. I sharply inhaled as I contemplated her question.

"How is it with my soul?" I repeated the question back to her. "I don't know that anyone has ever asked me that question. I don't even know where to begin."

"Well, now is the time for you to listen to your soul," she replied. "It's yearning to be heard."

And then we sat in silence. For the next thirty minutes, I sat in a room with my spiritual director, contemplating this question.

I didn't leave that day with an answer. In typical Rozella fashion, I asked questions about the first question that was asked of me. How am I supposed to know how my soul is? What questions do I ask of it? How do I hear from it? What is my soul and where does it even reside?

I found myself in this spiritual director's office that day because my life was falling apart. My husband and I were separating. I was employed by a church and struggling with one of the pastors who was my supervisor. My family was in Houston and I was in Atlanta, trying to keep it all together even as chaos swirled around me. I was in therapy, finally medicated for my depression and anxiety, and engaging in physical activity. But something was still off, and I couldn't put my finger on it. One of my friends suggested that I visit a spiritual director. I figured it couldn't hurt, so off I went to a local Episcopal church that offered spiritual direction.

How is it with your soul?

I began to realize that this question couldn't be answered in a traditional way. There were no right or simple answers and no glaring clues to lead me to the discovery of how my soul was faring. Rather, this question invited me to stillness and the quieting of my entire being—of my heart, body, mind, and soul—in order to uncover what was always present but never engaged. There is something about getting really quiet and really still. It makes it harder to hide from things that you don't want to deal with or ignore the feelings that have been deeply buried. The thought of doing this work scared me at first. I wasn't sure what I would find. I don't think I had ever sat quietly with myself and paid attention to my inner life.

How is it with your soul?

Over the course of that year, I met with my spiritual director twice a month and we reflected on this question and many others. I came to see that I hadn't attended to my soul at any point in my life, and now, it was hiding from me. I was called into a space that I had never been, the space of soul work. It was time for me to go on a journey to seek out my soul, to lure her out of her hiding place, and to care for her.

Back to the Beginning

I remember the word *soul* being used in three contexts when I was growing up. First, as a Black person growing up in a Black household, we often referenced the soul. Soul food, soul music, and *Soul Train* were all a part of my formation. In this context, having soul meant embodying a level of Blackness and cultural pride that connected to our past. Soul food was the food of our ancestors, food that was often made from scraps or whatever was accessible. The level of love and care that was put into the food made it soulful. Music that tapped into the essence of the Black experience—that encompassed the depths of pain, the joy that was an act of resistance, and the hope for a better tomorrow—was soulful. *Soul Train* was a television show that incorporated soul music with dancing that was native to the Black community. You could turn on *Soul Train* and see people who looked like you, wearing hairstyles that white society often deemed unacceptable, moving bodies that were often commodified or denigrated. *Soul Train* celebrated Blackness in ways that combined popular music, fashion, and culture.

The second context I experienced the word *soul* in was the area of relationships. I often heard the term *soul mate* used to refer to people who were connected across time and space—to people who had an indescribable energy that drew them to each other. I sensed early on that your soul mate was the person who connected to something deeper than your outer being; they were attracted to the essence of who you were, and their soul spoke to yours. Since I loved romance, this concept intrigued me, probably to a fault. I searched for my soul mate, for the one who would complete me, à la Jerry Maguire. It would take me almost thirty years to realize that this was a flawed concept.

Soul also came up in a third context, one that was a bit confusing and took me a while to figure out: religion. Growing up in a mainline, progressive church, I didn't hear much talk about the soul from a religious perspective. I can remember hymns that referenced it, but I don't recall specific conversations or lessons about the soul. I was an active participant, going to church every Sunday, attending youth group, singing in the youth choir, and serving the community regularly. I was nurtured by faithful adults in the church who took seriously my faith formation. And yet, the soul was not something that we discussed. If I'm honest, the only reference to the soul that I can recall coming across when I was a child is from the Shema (the most essential prayer in Judaism and an important Scripture passage for Christians as well):

> Hear, O Israel: The Lord our God, the Lord is one.
> Love the Lord your God with all your heart and
> with all your soul and with all your strength.[2]

This was the only teaching about the soul I can remember, and it really didn't teach me anything. I figured that the soul was a part of my being, but as for its function or importance? I had no clue. It wasn't until I got older, around high school, that I engaged in conversations about the soul with friends who went to religiously conservative churches. For the first time in my life, I heard people talking about the soul in the context of faith, and it wasn't pretty. My friends were focused on making sure that their soul was "right with God" to avoid burning in hell for eternity. During most of these conversations, I was at a complete loss. I felt like I had missed a whole lesson on the dos and don'ts of the soul. Why would someone's soul burn in hell? What does it mean for one's soul to be "right with God"? What kind of God did my friends believe in that would lead them to make a statement like this? What did I miss?

I knew that answering the question posed to me by my spiritual director would require me to dig deep and uncover what I had forgotten I knew about my soul. Even though my formative experiences introduced me to her, I didn't really know her. Being introduced to something is not the same as knowing something. When we know something, we do the work to nurture it. After years of not caring for my soul, I found myself sitting with a spiritual director in my midtwenties, wondering who my soul was, how she was, and why she even mattered.

Based on my formative experiences, I knew that the soul dealt with the essence of a person. My essence as a Black woman, my essence as a lover, my essence as a person of faith—all of these connect back to the soul. In order for my soul to be restored, I had to be restored. I had to delve into the depths of who I was, how I loved, and what mattered most to me. Each of these pointed to a deeper level of understanding, one that led me to listen to my inner voice of wisdom. Slowly, I began to truly know my soul and listen to how she was.

The Soul of Black Folks

During the first twenty years of my life, my Blackness was constantly called into question. This always baffled me. Clearly, I'm Black. But my Blackness was questioned by my family, by my friends, and even by white folks in a way that led me to believe that I embodied the wrong "type" of Blackness. With my family, I was teased because I was raised differently than both of my parents. They were from urban environments and faced challenges that were typical of Black folks living in urban centers. My father was from a housing community in Harlem and my mother, while she lived in a single-family home, was from a part of Jamaica, Queens, that was riddled with gangs. Some of her closest friends were gang members and drug kingpins, but that's a story for another time.

My parents' relationships and their lived experiences gave them a particular angle of vision regarding Blackness. In their minds, to be Black was to be street savvy and soulful, using particular language and resonating with stories that were a part of the Black experience in the United States. My dad's family was poor, and my mom's family was working class. For better or for worse, Blackness tends to be aligned with socioeconomic realities. The contexts of my parents' formation colored their views of Blackness.

I wasn't raised in the same environment as my parents. My family relocated from New York to Texas, moving to a suburb of Houston when I was six years old. The suburb we moved to was primarily Black, and I attended all-Black schools—elementary, middle, and high school. Being a suburbanite and not having the same experiences as my parents led to some teasing from my family, which impacted how I viewed myself. I often wondered what made me "less Black" in the eyes of my family. I can remember thinking that I went to all-Black primary and secondary schools and a Historically Black College and University (HBCU) and majored in urban sociology and with a minor in African studies. In my mind, I couldn't be anything but Black! My father recently apologized for teasing me when I was younger. He said it was his own ignorance that led him to believe that Blackness could only be embodied and expressed in one way.

My peers also questioned my Blackness. I was teased for how I spoke, often told that I "sounded white." My penchant for reading and, quite frankly, being a nerd didn't help my social standing before high school. When my family first moved to Houston, I wore my hair in styles that were prominent in the North but seen as out of place in the South. Looking back, I find it ironic because the hairstyles and clothing I wore, while unpopular, were most certainly Black! Whether it was my braids or my Kente cloth sneakers, I reflected a certain type of Blackness, though it wasn't always the most popular.

It wasn't until I graduated from high school that I spent more and more time in primarily white communities. In these places, I found that the Blackness I embodied was surprising to many. I would get complimented on my "articulateness." I was often told that my demeanor was refreshing or altogether surprising. I remember once while leading an event, I was pulled aside by a white woman who asked if I went to college. She was seemingly impressed. The questioning of my Blackness by white folks initially irritated me and eventually it enraged me. In these unsolicited comments and questions, I was reminded that who I was and how I showed up was surprising and not reflective of the Blackness they imagined. In these moments, I was reminded of the concept of *double consciousness*, coined by W. E. B. Du Bois, one of the United States' earliest sociologists. He said,

> One ever feels his twoness,—an American, a Negro; two souls, two thoughts, two unreconciled strivings; two warring ideals in one dark body, whose dogged strength alone keeps it from being torn asunder.[3]

So much of my life had been moving between two worlds—a Black world and a white world. I was never really at home in the Black world and certainly not at home in the white world. I was constantly questioning who I was at my core and how I should show up in the world.

Questioning my Blackness led to a disconnection from my very soul, from the essence of who I was. I was not only experiencing double consciousness, I was trying to figure out who I was. When your existence is ridiculed or questioned, it can lead you to wonder who you are and how you should show up in the world. At its worst, it can lead you to believe that you aren't worthy and valuable. I believe that some of the decisions I made when I was younger were directly tied to this disconnection. When you don't know who you are, you are constantly trying to find yourself in other people and experiences. This led to a lot of pain and years wandering in the proverbial wilderness.

Then, in 2007, I journeyed to Kenya with a group from the Awakenings Movement—a faith-based community I was a part of in Houston, Texas. I was twenty-five years old and preparing to go to seminary that fall. The trip was for young adults from the United States to meet with young adults throughout Kenya, learning from them and discovering how faith and spirituality were practiced in their context. I fell in love with the people and the places, but one experience has stayed with me and brought me into contact with a soul that had been struggling to find her center.

This was my second time to the continent, and I was once again overwhelmed by the feeling of being surrounded by Blackness. Whenever I go to Africa, I am in awe of the people—entire countries are made up of people who look just like me. That is transformative for a person who was not raised in a society where her Blackness is the norm. One Sunday, we worshipped with an amazing community in a rural area outside of Nairobi. Worship was unlike anything I had experienced. Thousands of people were gathered in a makeshift worship building. We were crowded onto benches and it was hot. The air wasn't moving, but the Spirit was alive and well. Music was played, and women wore beautiful clothing, singing and dancing their praises to God. It never ceases to amaze me that no matter where I worship around the world, if the Spirit is present, I don't need to speak the language. She moves in and out of people in ways that make a space come to life. I kept looking at those gathered and wondering, "Are these my people? Am I descended from Kenyans?"

Like many Black Americans, I know very little about my lineage. I can trace my mother's side of the family to the Caribbean, but the ancestry information for my father's family was lost in the cruel chaos of the transatlantic slave trade. I minored in African studies because I was fascinated with a place and a people who had been to hell and back. As I sat and worshipped with the community, tears welled up and silently spilled over. There was something happening in my soul that I could not explain, something that was drawing me out of a wilderness I had been wandering through.

After the service, our group was invited to meet with the pastor and elders of the church. We crowded into his office and were offered coffee and tea. Our group leader introduced us, and we settled in for a time of listening and sharing. The conversation was riveting as the leaders shared their joys, struggles, and hopes for their community. We learned about their hardships and their resilience in the face of difficulty and despair. As the conversation came to an end, our group leader asked a final question.

"What should we tell our friends and family back home? What messages from you and from this country should we deliver?"

The pastor leaned back in his chair and steepled his hands. After a moment of silence, he said, "You should remind your people in the United States that you, Black Americans, are the ones who made it. Your ancestors survived the Middle Passage. They lived through slavery and Reconstruction. They changed the country with the Civil Rights Movement. The blood that runs through your veins is the blood of those who made it."

After he said this, you could have heard a pin drop. All of us were staring at him, rapt. Tears were streaming down our faces, and for the first time, I realized what my Blackness means to me. It means that I am a survivor in the face of incomprehensible circumstances. I realized that the identity I was seeking could be found in the stories and history of my people, of our struggles, our triumphs, and our desire for a better life. I came face to face with my essence. The souls of the Black folks that had come before me, in their varied expressions and experiences, were calling me to embrace my Blackness and find rest for my soul in the knowledge that I was enough. And glorious.

Once I came to this revelation, I was ready to meet my soul mate. Except, it didn't happen the way I expected.

Soul Mates

For most of my life, I only thought about soul mates in terms of romantic relationships. I never thought about soul mates in the context of platonic relationships. I don't know if it's cultural expectations or my own romantic sensibilities, but I conflated *soul mate* and *lifelong romantic partner* in ways that were unhealthy and probably added too much pressure on my intimate relationships.

A soul mate is a person who loves us to life, seeing all of who we are and choosing to show up every day because we matter. They are people who love us in spite of ourselves and reflect God's love, grace, and commitment to us in real time. Soul mates can appear in any number of contexts, and you know you've found one when your soul leaps with joy—and you'll likely find many soul mates throughout your life. You know you're with your soul mate when you experience comfort and a peace that surpasses all understanding. I met my soul mate, Esther, when I was in seminary and life had taken an unforeseen turn.

Esther and I met during a time of unbecoming in my life. I had relocated from Houston to Philadelphia in the fall of 2007 and was planning a wedding for January 2008. I was a first-year seminarian, living in a city that I did not like, trying to be a wife and partner, and dealing with my depression. It was a dark time, but Esther became a light in the darkness. Esther and I got to know each other and became friends on a trip to Egypt in January of 2009. Traveling together has a way of revealing the true nature of a relationship, and we learned that we were meant to be after this experience.

Esther and I understand each other in ways I cannot fully explain. I know myself and the baggage that I bring. She sees me, my baggage, and my roller coaster of emotions and welcomes us in, without any question. Even though we come from very different backgrounds, we have very similar values. We care deeply about God's people and believe in the power of faith and spirituality to heal and transform the world. Esther and I believe that laughter is the best medicine. So much of our time together is spent laughing—at ourselves, at each other, at anything that brings us joy.

We are complicated women, and both of us accept the other fully. I know without a shadow of a doubt that Esther will be in my life until death do us part. I never have to be anyone other than who I am when I'm with Esther. She gets my corny nature. She calls me out on my bullshit. She loves me unconditionally.

My friendship with Esther taught me that soul mates are real and that they come in all forms. Esther reflects back to me a God who is faithful and deeply passionate about people. Her presence in my life beckons my soul out from its hiding place because she is safe and secure and loving. That's how I know she's my soul mate. The essence of who I am longs to be around her and seeks to be seen. She reminds me to listen to the inner voice of wisdom, the voice of my soul desperately trying to be heard.

Connecting with your soul's mate requires that you be open—open to being completely seen, heard, and known. And I don't know about you, but for me, this is terrifying. Esther and I met at a time when my soul was beckoning me to stop and listen. We met at a time when life was chaotic, but I was committed to finding peace in the whirlwind. Discovering your soul's mate requires that you be attentive to what your soul needs and who is around you. God uses us to speak life to one another, but we are so busy that we miss God's invitation to be seen and loved just for who we are.

Stop. Listen. Feel. Look. This is how we become aware of our soul's mate. We become still and listen to the voice within. I believe there is power to voicing our requests. If you are in need of your soul's mate, ask for it. Then, allow yourself to really feel, paying attention to what comes to the surface and recognizing what you need. And look around, surveying your environment for those who God might be using to speak to you. We find our soul's mate when we open ourselves up to be found. But first we have to be still.

Soulful(l) Restoration

In the spring of 2013, I was sitting in my beautiful condo overlooking Lake Michigan in Chicago. I had an incredible job as a program director for one of the largest Protestant denominations in the United States. I was good at my job and had built an impressive reputation in my field. By all accounts, I was living a great life. I traveled all around the world, engaged in meaningful work, had incredible friends, was clear about who I was and whose I was, and even had a few soul mates to boot! But something still wasn't right. Something was off. And then, Beyoncé released her visual album *Lemonade*.

I was watching the much-anticipated premiere alone with a glass of wine. I had been on the road the week prior and was in desperate need of some downtime. So many things were unfolding in our culture and in my community that I just needed a moment to breathe. I was still reeling from incidents from the year before—the massacre of nine beloved souls by a young adult with an affiliation to a Lutheran church and my subsequent public post calling out the church (more on this in chapter 8)—and was trying to find a moment of peace and calm. As I settled in to view what has become a cultural phenomenon, I was not ready for the array of emotions and level of resonance I would feel as I watched her masterpiece.

I don't think people understand how meaningful Beyoncé is to Black women. Who she is, how she nurtures her craft, where she places her time and energy, the ways that she uses her creativity, her unapologetic boundaries, and her ongoing commitment to evolution and excellence continue to astound me. She makes us want to be the best version of ourselves without inducing jealousy or a desire to be anything or anyone other than who we are. In *Lemonade*, I witnessed a woman who had faced heartbreak and pain. By tapping into her vulnerability, she created her best piece of work yet. She shared a story of a woman moving from devastation, through the unknown, to redemption. This wasn't an easy journey, and it required sacrifice, hard work, forgiveness, and self-love. As I watched her story unfold, I began to cry. My soul recognized something that I hadn't been able to articulate or describe.

Up until that moment, I was living a life that wasn't mine. I was doing good and faithful work, but it wasn't the work that God ultimately created me for. I had neglected the lessons of my past and was not keeping my soul, the essence of who I am, front and center. I knew this to be true because I didn't feel grounded. There was a continual rub between my identity and my values and the work I was called to do. I didn't feel like I could be my full self, with my soul front and center. I lacked peace and joy.

Watching Beyoncé's story made me reflect on my own story. I had been running from the truth that was staring me in the face—the work and the community I had pledged allegiance too wasn't the space where God was calling me to serve. And this was a devastating realization. I spoke to my dad that night, sharing with him my hurt and my struggles. I wanted to come home, but I was terrified of walking away from the life I had built. Even when I knew what I needed to do, there was still a feeling of fear that was present. My doubts rose to the surface as I considered walking away from it all and listening to my soul, to the deepest desire that kept begging to be free.

I spent the next week in prayer, calling on my friends to pray with and for me. I needed clarity and guidance. I wanted to make sure I was listening to the inner voice of wisdom. I had been out of practice, and, truthfully, I didn't trust myself to make the right decision. I needed a community praying with me during this time of discernment. At that moment, a forgotten question rose to the surface. "Rozella, how is it with your soul?"

I was able to respond openly and honestly that my soul was in need of some attention and nourishment, that my soul had been neglected and was seeking restoration.

The first step was to be still. To stop moving and literally sit with myself. I had been running so hard and so fast for so long that my being was cluttered. My essence was impeded because I wouldn't sit still.

In that moment, I realized what I was missing. I was missing an integrated existence, one that called me to live with an awakened mind, a repaired heart, a reformed body, and a restored soul. I had been a living cognitive dissonance—creating a life that was externally lauded but was not internally reflective of who God created me to be or my deepest desires. I wasn't living a soulful life, nor was my soul full.

I made the decision to leave my job and return home. It was a risky decision. At that time I didn't have a plan for what was next, but I knew that I had to listen to my soul. It never ceases to amaze me that once we let go of whatever it is we are holding on to, other paths and opportunities are revealed. When I honored my soul and made the decision to leave my job, I experienced a peace unlike any I had encountered before.

Restoring my soul is probably the hardest work I've ever done because it requires me to be excruciatingly honest with myself and to listen deeply and well. Stripping away the shoulds of your life and listening to the voice within that reveals who you are, what you value, what brings you joy, and how you are called to bring that joy to life is hard. Letting go of others' expectations of you and deciding to live for yourself and your God is not easy. But that's the invitation. That's the work that's needed to be done in order to experience restoration. And the people who you are in soulful relationship with are the people who will support you during this time. Revolutionary relationships will encourage you to listen to your soul and will reflect back to you that which God would have you know. So listen carefully. And listen well. Restoration is in store for you.

CHAPTER 7

Revolutionary Relationships Defined

God for us, God alongside us, God within us.[1]

revolutionary (adjective): Involving or causing a
    complete or dramatic change
relationship (noun): The state of being connected
revolutionary relationship: A connection defined
    by creativity, liberation, and sustainability
    that leads to the complete transformation of
    a person and a community

Not every relationship is revolutionary. These are not just loving relationships or long-lasting relationships. Revolutionary relationships change the people involved for the better and have the power to push people outside the confines of private relationships in ways that have public implications. Revolutionary relationships lead to healing and transformation and are rooted in the reality of God's own revolutionary relationship—the Trinity.

God in Relationship with God

As a Christian, I believe in one God who exists in three forms—a complex concept! Many wonder how Christians can claim to be monotheists—those who articulate faith in one God—and yet refer to God as three different entities. Much ink has been spilled by theologians over the centuries, attempting to make sense of this theological paradox—that God could be both three and one. Instead of spending my time in philosophical arguments, I've chosen to pay attention to what God in relationship with Godself could teach me about my relationships. The Trinity is a fundamental way of being that God has modeled for humanity. When I stopped trying to understand the Trinity for the sake of proving its validity and focused on the meaning that the Trinity presented for me and my relationships, I began a journey of discovery.

When ordinary people connect, truly seeing, knowing, and loving one another, extraordinary moments come to life. The Trinity is the embodiment of relationship, of connection. God in the Trinity models revolutionary relationship in ways that show what life could be like when we fall in love with ourselves and each other.

God is love, and the first act of this life-giving love was to create the world. When the Creator formed the earth and her inhabitants, the love of God was imprinted on every field and flow, within every creature and tree. The love of God crafted humans in the *imago Dei*, breathing life into our very form so that we could reflect this love within ourselves and toward others. God looked upon it all and proclaimed that it was good. When we pay close attention to the life all around us, we bear witness to the love of God in action.

The second act of love that God enacts is that of liberation. To liberate is to set one free from oppression of any type. Jesus is God as liberator. In the Christian story, God joins with humanity in a way that the Divine had not done before. The second entity of the Trinity is Jesus, the one who came to liberate humanity from ways of being that separated us from God. When God became Emmanuel—God with us—the Divine entered into the most intimate relationship with humanity, becoming us so that we could be known, seen, and loved fully. God chose a relationship with us defined not by hierarchy but by a challenge to any system of belief that divides people from each other.

In Jesus, we see a God who models love and community. Jesus calls us back to God and to each other by highlighting what matters most—how we love God, ourselves, and each other. Jesus's life provides a roadmap for liberation. It is astounding in its simplicity, and yet we continually miss the mark and go off course. As an act of love, God became human to show us what a liberated existence could be and reminds us constantly that it's for everyone. No one should be without the opportunity to experience liberation.

In the third act of love, God makes good on an everlasting promise to never leave or forsake creation. The Holy Spirit was given to us to continually pull us out of ourselves and call us to practice presence in the world, with our hearts and souls tuned in to the holy in our midst. It is nothing but an act of love to leave a part of yourself with another, to leave your light and Divine energy behind in order for people to remember who and whose they are. This is what God does with the Holy Spirit, and this action sustains us in our day-to-day lives as we love ourselves and each other. The power of the Holy Spirit makes revolutionary relationships possible and sustains them.

The Trinity provides an embodied example of a revolutionary relationship. It shows us how love is practiced and gives us a way forward, a way marked by creativity, liberation, and sustainability. When relationships model these characteristics, restoration, healing, and wholeness become possible, not just for individuals but also for communities.

Lessons from the Trinity

The simplest things can sometimes be the most difficult to practice. If we start with the Trinity as the ultimate model of revolutionary relationships, we get a clear pathway into love, into relationships that are life-giving and transformative. But life is more complex than this, and we often get in our own way. Instead of following the example laid out before us, we are quick to believe that life will be easier if we turn inward and focus on ourselves in ways that are not reflective of the love that God has called us to. We don't practice relationship with an eye toward creativity and liberation.

God's choice to relate to us as creator, liberator, and sustainer is a choice full of risk and challenge. God has given us room as humans to act freely in the world, and we so often act against our best interests and against God's will for us. And yet, because God relates to us as Trinity, God is an accompanying presence rather than an external one. In the Trinity, God shifts closer to us to understand who we are.

Revolutionary relationships are hard *and* good. They take work and are not for the faint of heart. With every act of the Trinity, God engages in hard work— creating, liberating, and sustaining us. God takes time with us and trusts us, working in each of us toward a larger purpose to bring about healing. Revolution- ary relationships demand that we fall in love with our- selves and with each other. We are invited into each other's lives in ways that we are unaccustomed to. No conversation is off limits. Everything is on the table to be discussed, reflected upon, or challenged. A relationship is hard and good when the challenges that we experience in the context of the relationship lead us to deeper awareness and connection. This is what the Trinity teaches us—to come closer and go deeper, even when it's hard.

Goodness pervades our entire being when we do the hard work of loving ourselves and each other: relationships are restored, people are healed, communities bind together and experience wholeness, ensuring that every need is met, and we all experience joy and peace.

Not only are revolutionary relationships hard and good, they *are based on a covenant mentality; are life-giving, risk-taking, vulnerable, forgiving, gracious, and diverse; and hold us accountable.*

Covenant, Not Commitment

A friend of mine taught me an important distinction between a commitment and a covenant.[2]

A commitment is a contract that can be broken, allowing both sides to walk away from the relationship. While there might be consequences, a commitment only must be kept if both parties or entities in the relationship decide to keep it. A covenant, on the other hand, is not dependent on what the other person does or doesn't do. God is the ultimate example of a covenant maker. God made a covenant with humanity, and it is not broken when we fall short. God continues to keep the promises made in spite of what we do.

Because we are humans, and not God, it's important to remember that sometimes walking away from a relationship is the right choice, especially if it is life-taking. *If a relationship does violence to your being—your mind, your heart, your soul, or your body—you have every right to walk away. Full stop.*

In the context of healthy relationships, thinking about commitment versus covenant is helpful. When I first heard it, I immediately harkened back to my marriage. I am now divorced, and I realized, some six years later, that I entered my marriage based on commitment and not on covenant. I didn't make promises that I would keep despite what my husband did or didn't do. I made an agreement that could be easily broken because I didn't view it as a covenant. Whether I did or didn't show up was based on what he did or didn't do. All of my actions were dependent on his actions, and this led to a cycle of hurt, disappointment, shame, and disconnection. This wasn't the only reason for the demise of our marriage, and I don't solely blame myself, but I can honestly say that this way of thinking did more harm than good.

My female friendships have helped me understand what relationships based on a covenant mentality actually look like. While we aren't God and we fall short, our relationships aspire to be covenantal. The group of women friends I refer to as my soul sisters and the hedge of protection love me in spite of myself and reflect a God who sees and knows who I really am. These are revolutionary relationships, in which I am invited to intentionally and purposefully live out my values. We have conversations about what matters most and how we want to show up in this world. Our relationship isn't dependent on what I do or don't do. I am loved regardless. Within the context of our covenant, we continually show up, without keeping record of rights and wrongs. We trust each other and believe that the relationship will last regardless of what might happen in this life.

Life-Giving

Revolutionary relationships give life. They don't take life. God the Lover is about creating, liberating, and sustaining life. An experience is life-giving when it uplifts your spirit and nurtures joy in your life. Relationships that are life-giving lead to holistic growth and are concerned with the well-being of both parties. If a relationship is not life-giving, it is not revolutionary.

I've been in so many relationships that were soul-crushing. You know you are not in a life-giving relationship when you constantly feel defeated, like anything you say or do isn't enough; when you feel like the success of your relationship is entirely dependent on you. You also know you're not in a life-giving relationship if you feel like you can't bring your full self to the relationship. Life-giving relationships want all of you to show up, without apology.

When I didn't love myself or believe that I deserved to be in relationships that were life-giving, I continually chose to engage people who drained my energy. This created an unhealthy cycle that left me worse off after each relationship ended. The most telling sign that you are in a relationship that is not life-giving is if the other person is not interested in their own growth and personal development. A relationship simply cannot nurture life if the participants are not nurturing life within themselves.

I believe in a God who honors life so much that God not only created life but chose to embody life as well. This life was creative and in relationship. The God of life does not approach us from a place of isolation but is communal in nature. Revolutionary relationships mirror this value when both parties constantly seek out life and believe that life overcomes death, at every turn.

Risk-Taking

With creation, God took a risk. We were not created to be unthinking, noncreative beings. God gave us free will and told us that we had dominion over the entirety of creation. I often wonder if this risk was worth it given the sad state of affairs we are in. Nevertheless, God took a risk on us at the beginning of creation and again at the incarnation. It was a risk of the highest proportion to become human, and humanity responded by torturing and murdering the embodiment of God's hope for humanity. Even still, I believe that risk-taking is integral to revolutionary relationships.

Loving and trusting one another is the biggest risk most of us will ever take. It requires that we let go of control and let ourselves be fully seen and known. It requires vulnerability, which I will touch on in a moment. It asks that we lean in when everything in us wants to pull back because we believe that the risk is too great to bear. But here's the thing: without taking the risk, we can't experience the fullness of life. Without the risk of becoming human, we wouldn't know what it means to love God, love ourselves, and love our neighbors well. We wouldn't know what community centered on justice, mercy, humility, and love actually looks like. We wouldn't have a model for welcoming all people and creating an inclusive movement that seeks to turn systems upside down, focusing more on the well-being of people than on the accumulation of resources. When I consider the risk that God took in becoming human through this lens, I absolutely believe it was worth it.

Vulnerable

The dominant Western culture demonizes vulnerability. It is looked down upon and seen as a weakness. I've come to think of vulnerability as a gift and not as a weakness. This has been affirmed in recent years as the work of Dr. Brené Brown has gained notoriety. She invites us all to revisit our beliefs around shame, vulnerability, and courage.[3]

Embracing vulnerability requires that we come to terms with some truths:

- There is a very real possibility that you will be hurt.
- When you choose to be vulnerable, you invite others to do the same.
- When we are in revolutionary relationships, our vulnerability allows us to move from the shallow to the deep.

Vulnerability seems counterintuitive for so many of us. To let down our guard and to open ourselves up to the possibility of being hurt or taken advantage of is incredibly difficult. The strategies we've cultivated to protect ourselves from hurt have enabled us to survive, especially if we have experienced trauma of any kind. But these strategies may not be what we need to move to the next chapter of our lives. It may be time to take on new practices and ways of being that invite closeness rather than sustain distance. Maybe we need to let go of those things that protect us from others so we can grow in relationship rather than letting our fear push us away. Revolutionary relationships invite us to take on a new way of being, one where vulnerability is considered a strength and not a weakness.

A relationship is revolutionary when both parties practice vulnerability. It's reciprocal and not one-sided. When reciprocity is not a part of the relationship, one person carries the brunt of the emotional labor. Practicing vulnerability takes courage and continually invites us to deepen our trust in each other. Think back to a relationship where you felt like you were always giving of yourself, your time, your resources, your energy. Where you felt like you were carrying the relationship on your own. Where your needs and desires were not taken into account. I'm guessing you can think of one. This was not a relationship built on reciprocity. Relationships that are reciprocal are relationships that embody equality. There isn't a hierarchy in the relationship and each participant is concerned about the needs, desires, and hopes of the other.

So many of our relationships are transactional rather than reciprocal. We enter into relationships with the hopes of gaining something or with the expectation that the other person can do something for us. Once we get what we want from the relationship, we end it. If we don't get what we want, we go looking for another relationship to fill our needs.

Revolutionary relationships practice reciprocal vulnerability and invite each person in the relationship to a place of sharing, giving, and receiving. People share their desires, give what the other needs, and receive from another. The cycle continues on until it becomes a way of life, until people no longer apologize for asking for what they need and are able to receive without feeling the need to respond.

Forgiveness

My faith teaches me daily about forgiveness. God is constantly forgiving humanity and inviting us to forgive one another. Hurting another and being hurt in the context of relationship are inevitable. We are broken people, and broken people hurt people.

And here's the thing about pain: regardless of whether you are hurt maliciously or unintentionally, pain is still pain. When someone breaks our heart, when we experience profound disappointment, when our dreams and hopes are dashed, when someone intentionally seeks our demise, we experience suffering. I don't believe that God causes suffering, but I do believe that God is with us in the midst of our pain. In the incarnation, God experienced what it is to be a human, so God can empathize with us in every experience of pain.

There aren't many things that Jesus says point blank. I sometimes get mad because Jesus taught more in parables and with metaphors than he did with clear-cut, black-and-white answers. However, Jesus was very clear about forgiveness in the Christian Bible. Throughout the Gospels, Jesus taught that forgiveness was a necessity to being in right relationship. Revolutionary relationships practice forgiveness—choose forgiveness—over and over again.

To be clear, the act of forgiveness is also reciprocal. A relationship that doesn't embody reciprocity is not a revolutionary relationship. I also believe that forgiveness happens with the aid of a power outside of ourselves. Forgiveness cannot be demanded, it has to be invited in when a person is ready to let go of the pain that the broken relationship has caused.

Gracious

Revolutionary relationships remind us that we are human. We are invited to practice grace, which begins when we give people the benefit of the doubt, believing the best in them rather than the worst in them. Grace is defined as unmerited favor. Practicing grace in our relationships is countercultural. People are supposed to earn affection, respect, and our trust. To be gracious is to reject the narrative that these things must be earned and to practice freely giving them instead.

Here's what I've learned: I am only as gracious to another person as I am toward myself. Grace begets grace. When I freely give myself affection, respect, and trust, I am better able to do that for others. Practicing grace is a lifetime endeavor. We are not perfect, and we will fail. But like anything else, the more we practice, the better we become and our mentality shifts. We become less suspicious of others. We lead with compassion and a true desire to understand rather than with judgment. We recognize that most people are doing the best that they can on any given day, ourselves included, and we give people a break.

Diverse

I would not be the woman I am without the diversity of relationships in my life. I've always been someone who nurtured relationships with people from a variety of backgrounds. This might be connected to the fact that I am from a diverse family, but it also is something I do intentionally. I put myself in spaces and places where I can seek out those who are different from me in order to be in relationship. When I talk about diversity, I am not just talking about racial and ethnic diversity. I am talking about diversity of thought, economic background, identity, orientation, religious affiliation (or lack thereof), geographic location, educational attainment—you name it! One of the greatest blessings in my life is to be engaged in diverse relationships.

Diversity by itself is not what's most important. And diversity for diversity's sake doesn't cut it. When I talk about diversity, I mean a space where we aren't expected to water down, assimilate, or integrate our identities (particularly those of us with marginalized identities). We pride ourselves on valuing diversity, but oftentimes what we really value is representation, not authentic relationship. We don't honor the image of God in a person if we expect them to ignore or diminish aspects of their identity in order to fit in.

If you are not engaging in diverse relationships, you are missing out on a depth of connection, awareness, and experience. We miss out on God's creativity when we surround ourselves with people who are just like us. Being in authentic relationships with those who are different from you will also teach you more about yourself. I've come to understand my beliefs and values in a deeper way because of revolutionary relationships that embody diversity.

Accountable

Revolutionary relationships hold each person involved in the relationship accountable—accountable to who they say they want to be, what they say they value, and how they show up in the world. For me, this is the hardest aspect of being in a revolutionary relationship. Not only do I have to be vulnerable and forgiving, but I have to be open to critique. I have to accept that the relationship will challenge me for the better.

I used to really dislike being held accountable, but I've come to realize that it's not necessarily accountability that I dislike, it's accountability without a relationship. I need to know that the person challenging me has my best interest at heart. It's also important to me that anyone who is challenging me is also doing the hard work of learning and loving themselves. The goal of accountability in the context of revolutionary relationships is not to dictate another's behavior. The goal is to name your hopes, values, and dreams, claim the ways that you want to show up in the world, and have a partner that helps you do the good and hard work of staying focused on the fact that what you say matters most.

Without accountability, I would not be where I am today. Without people in my life calling me out when my values and my actions are misaligned, I would not be the person I am today. Revolutionary relationships invite participants to hold each other accountable as they seek out restoration, healing, and wholeness.

The Foundation

Revolutionary relationships create the foundation for building lives of meaning, joy, connection, and love. They also have the power to heal us, as individuals and as communities. Revolutionary relationships remind us that we belong to one another. And this reminder leads us to live and love in ways that shift the world around us. There is a profound correlation between our quality of life and the quality of our relationships. Now more than ever, we need revolutionary relationships.

CHAPTER 8

Love Big, Heal the World

The key to creating health is figuring out the
cause of the problem and then providing the right
conditions for the body and soul to thrive.
—Dr. Mark Hyman[1]

Cleaning the Wound

I've spent a lot of time in hospitals, working as a research assistant at one of the hospitals in the Texas Medical Center the summer before my junior year in high school, serving as a hospital chaplain for a year in Atlanta, and caring for relatives after major procedures that required long hospital stays. Hospitals have taught me so much about the creativity of the human mind, the strength of the human heart, the power of the human body, and the resilience of the human spirit. Some of the most important lessons of my life I learned from hospitals, patients, and medical professionals.

One of the most profound lessons came when I took the time to understand the science behind wound care and healing. From witnessing hospital staff care for a patient with burns to watching my father provide wound care for my grandmother, I learned that the healing process is painful, long, and requires intentional care. It often seemed as if things got worse before they got better, with the cleaning of the wound bringing about significant pain and discomfort.

Before healing can happen, cleaning the wound, also known as debridement, must take place. This is done to remove anything that stands in the way of healing—dead tissue or foreign objects found in the wound. Cleaning can include the use of chemicals, baths, and even scraping with instruments. I can remember holding my grandmother's hand as she had a leg wound debrided. It was painful and far from pretty. She suffered, and the wound looked worse before it got better.

Cleaning the wound can only happen when a patient is ready to accept that the wound exists and is in need of care. Until that moment, the wound festers and can lead to infection that, at worst, can kill a person. Only when a person is ready to get the care they need can the process of healing begin.

Humanity is sick, and this sickness has shown itself through the wounds of brokenness and disconnection. For so long, we have tried to ignore the wound, and it has gotten worse, spreading to healthy tissue and infecting our lives together. Foreign objects—here, the

-isms, including racism, sexism, classism, ableism—
have to be removed from our wounds for us to experience healing.

So many of us feel as if things are getting worse and
not better. We are wondering which news story or scien-
tific discovery or poverty statistic will finally be the one
that leads us to do something about our political leaders, climate change, and the lack of access to resources.
This book is an attempt to provide what's needed to
heal our wounds, but this can only happen if we are
willing to do the work. This work includes accepting our
woundedness, connecting to a creative, liberating, and
sustaining faith that can restore us, engaging the healing process by falling in love with our *whole* selves, and
forming revolutionary relationships.

At times in our history, we have attempted to clean
our communal wounds. Every time there's a justice
uprising, from the Civil Rights Movement to Black
Lives Matter to #MeToo, that's an attempt to clean our
wounds and seek healing. Leaders throughout history
have called out our wounds and turned our attention
to the deep-seated illness that threatens to overtake us.
There's momentum for the moment, but we often can't
sustain it because we haven't done the foundational
work of falling in love with ourselves and with each
other. We haven't engaged a life-giving faith that has
the power to sustain us. We rely on the emotions of a

moment to keep us committed to the eradication of the disease, but these emotions burn hot and fast.

Recognizing and cleaning the wound are the first steps, but that's not enough. In order to experience restoration, healing, and wholeness, we have to root out what is causing the disease in the first place. We have to engage a healing process to make sure that the wound fully heals and that healing isn't set back. This requires even more work, time, and intentional care. Without this time and care, amputation is the next option. Cutting away the diseased tissue to save the larger organism is a drastic measure that happens when the wound does not heal. And if that still doesn't work? Quality of life quickly deteriorates, and death is inevitable.

From Diseased to Well

I recently heard an episode of *The Marie Forleo Podcast* featuring Dr. Mark Hyman. This podcast is one of my favorites because it invites various people from diverse fields into conversation about their lives and how they've found meaning, connection, and success. In this particular episode, Hyman, the founder of the UltraWellness Center and the medical director at Cleveland Clinic's Center for Functional Medicine, described the concept of *functional medicine*, which was a new term to me. He explained that in our society, medicine has mainly served the purpose of curing disease rather than creating wellness. We treat people once they show signs of disease, but we don't pattern our health care around creating environments, practices, and beliefs that take into account the interdependent reality of our lives and biology. This leads us to constantly be behind the proverbial eight ball—we are always playing catch-up, focused more on the disease than the situations that caused the disease. We spend more time on Band-Aid solutions than we do on transforming people's beliefs and environments so that health flourishes.

This doesn't just apply to our health. Throughout our society, we tend to focus on short-term solutions rather than long-term well-being. In many spaces, especially within communities of faith, we aren't focused on creating and maintaining wellness. We are focused on the diseases and problems present in our contexts. We are more concerned with our declining numbers and resources than we are with the fact that people are fundamentally disconnected from themselves and each other. We are more concerned with our buildings and reputations than we are with the decreasing relevancy of our communities and practices. We would rather conserve a former way of being that we revere than creatively imagine and embody a new way, one that is more reflective of the diversity, inclusivity, and justice of God. We aren't focused on wellness or the prevention of disease; we are focused on staying afloat, ignoring the root causes of our problems.

I often wonder whether we even want to be made well. Do we know what wellness looks, feels, and sounds like? It's hard to imagine something if you've never experienced it or come into contact with its power. We can't begin the healing process if we don't admit our woundedness. Only then can we shift our focus from prevention to creation. Only then can we heal the world.

Healing the Wound

The wound-healing process includes four phases: hemostasis, inflammation, proliferation, and maturation.[2] Simply put, the first phase, hemostasis, is when the wound closes, which happens when blood clots. Inflammation is the second phase and happens when localized swelling occurs, which prevents infection and controls bleeding. Proliferation involves scabbing: the wound is rebuilt with new tissue and new blood vessels. Lastly, in the maturation phase, the wound fully closes. Scabs fall away and the skin, while healed, is weaker than it was to begin with.

This process has much to teach us when we think about our wounded world today. Ordinary moments present extraordinary solutions. We simply have to look at, listen to, and learn from the beauty and wisdom around us, which is divinely created and inspired by the Lover. Tapping back into God's power gives us the vision we need to see the world anew and view her through the lens of love rather than fear.

Using the wound-healing process as a guide, we have a roadmap for healing that changes us all.

Hemostasis—Stop the Bleeding

Blood is our life force. As long as it flows unencumbered and is not infected, it keeps us alive and well. We are currently bleeding out. Our life force is seeping out of us, and the bleeding must be stopped if we want our wounds to heal. This requires miraculous power, which can be tapped into when we turn our lives over to a God that wants nothing from us but love and love in action. This God, our faith, and love in action can make us well.

The bleeding is stopped when we deeply root ourselves into our creation story, into the story of life being made in the image of God. When God breathed into humanity, God gave us life. We stop the bleeding by applying the pressure of our faith, when we remember who and whose we are in ways that inspire us to call out anything and everything that tries to take our life force from us. This faith gives us the courage to stand up and speak out in the face of injustice.

Our blood clots when the collective community applies pressure on the forces that try to divide us from each other. We see it happening all around us today. There is a lot of injustice, *but* there is a lot of pressure. We are rising up, speaking up, and taking a stand against the injustice that threatens to rob us of our life force. Whatever the issue may be—violence against women and girls, police brutality, mass incarceration, income inequity, homelessness, the degradation of our planet—when we apply pressure to our wounds and take a stand, we experience healing. Engaging in creative acts that liberate ourselves and others provides sustenance for our lives together.

Inflammation—Protect the Area

Once we've stopped the bleeding, we continue to apply pressure, and we turn inward, rooting out anything that isn't uplifting, empowering, and nurturing within us. When I speak of protection here, I'm not talking about separating oneself in order to maintain a status quo. We protect ourselves and our communities by taking time to fall in love with ourselves. And with our faith as our guide, we begin to imagine a new reality.

This stage invites us into new ways of viewing ourselves and the world around us, but it is hard. Whenever we are required to change, we also enter a time of grieving—grieving who we were, what we believed, and sometimes relationships that were not meant for the next chapter of our life. In this stage, we seek out information that challenges previously held beliefs. We reflect on our lives, on what has formed and informed our thinking. We examine our thinking against a new, fundamental truth: God is the ultimate Lover, and we were created to love.

Do previously held ways of being and believing support this truth? If not, we sift and shift, asking for Divine guidance and connecting with others who are living out a love ethic. We address our own woundedness and the things that have broken our hearts. We make peace with our past, recognizing that we can't change what's happened. Our bodies become not just an arbitrary vessel but a reflection of the Divine—one that needs to be loved and nurtured in order to be well. And when we view our bodies in this way, we are led to see the humanity of others' bodies. Our souls come out of hiding, and we pay heed to their wisdom. Once we stop the bleeding, we do the work of connecting to ourselves. We then move outward to create a new reality.

Proliferation—Create a New Reality

A new reality is created when people engage in revolutionary relationships. Relationships that are life-giving, risk-taking, vulnerable, gracious, forgiving, diverse, and accountable have the power to make us well. But before they make us well, they challenge us to embody a different way of being.

When we engage in revolutionary relationships, we can no longer live life in a bubble of comfort or ignorance. By their very nature, these relationships draw us out of ourselves, leading us to care about the things that the people we are connected to care about. These relationships tilt our world on its axis. My relationships have not only enriched my core, they have led me to learn new lessons about life, love, joy, and pain. These relationships have opened me up to new sources of knowledge. I care about those who are Latinx, South Asian, LGBTQ; I care about the things that impact people who are not from my country; I care about populations that I've never lived with, simply because of these relationships. The people in my life have reflected God's Divine creativity, and by being in relationships with them, I have experienced God in new ways.

Not only do these relationships increase my knowledge and expand my compassion, they also lead me to action. I take up causes and speak out about things that impact the people that I am in relationship with, simply because I love them and because they bear the image of God. To not do so would be to turn my back on God.

Maturation—Live the New Reality

The healing process is complete when we put our values and our love into action. Each and every day we are called to make intentional choices that reflect the

Lover, our relationships, and the things that matter most. Every action and choice is measured against our new awareness and commitments. This is an incredibly difficult undertaking, and it's no wonder we haven't experienced true healing yet! But I do believe, without a shadow of a doubt, that it's possible.

The faith I profess points to a God who became human precisely to show us how to live within a new reality. In the incarnation, God shows us a level of love that we had not witnessed before. God sought us out, to be in revolutionary relationship with each of us, so that we could love big and find healing, together. This isn't easy and requires us to take some risks. I did that recently, and my life was forever changed.

Live Your Values

In April of 2016, I found myself at a crossroads. I was working for my denomination at the national headquarters, one year after Dylann Roof murdered nine Black people at Mother Emmanuel AME in Charleston, South Carolina. The massacre of Cynthia Marie Graham Hurd, Susie Jackson, Ethel Lee Lance, Depayne Middleton-Doctor, Clementa C. Pinckney, Tywanza Sanders, Daniel Simmons, Sharonda Coleman-Singleton, and Myra Thompson rocked me to my core. Not only did this tragic event happen on the heels of years of killings of

Black and brown people, it was perpetrated by a young white man who was affiliated with my denomination.

I was an outspoken leader in my denomination on issues of race and justice. I wrote about the massacre and how I felt being a Black member of a predominantly white denomination. I shared how my heart was broken after years of working toward racial justice and education in my denomination, only to find that we were raising white young adults who had the power and desire to violently kill people who look like me. I was exhausted. I was overwhelmed. I was heartbroken and had no idea what God was calling me to. I knew with every fiber of my being that my current role was no longer the right place for me. The work that I was doing did not reflect my deepest values.

Our bodies give us clues all the time. They tell us how we are feeling and what we need. I was paying attention to my body in ways I hadn't before—to the energy coursing through her and the emotions that were vibrating beneath the surface. During this time, a key thought kept emerging, "Rozella, you are not living out your values, and your body is suffering from this dissonance."

I knew that it was time to make a change. Was the work that I was doing inherently bad or wrong? No. But the work didn't reflect my identity or my values. When we become comfortable in our bodies, we begin to make decisions that honor who we are and what we value. We begin to live our values out loud, and that's when we see love in action.

Love in Action

> But love is really more of an interactive process. It's about what we do not just what we feel. It's a verb, not a noun.[3]

Do you remember the first time that love shifted in your life from being a noun to a verb? When love shifted from being merely a feeling to impassioned action that required intentional work and commitment? Do you remember when love became something that you'd fight to keep rather than a fleeting desire? Every revolutionary relationship represents this type of love—love as an interactive process. I have deep and abiding feelings of respect and compassion for the people in my life, but our relationships go beyond feelings. They move to a place deep within that is reflective of the love that God models for us in the incarnation. They represent a certain "withness," the constant presence of a person who has committed to me and our relationship. Revolutionary relationships lead me to action. I must nurture these relationships and the people I love. I can't be selfish because these relationships continually pull me out of myself and into the world.

That's what God's love did. God's love for humanity was so powerful that it pulled the Divine Being from the heavens and to earth, to be with us. In Jesus, we see a God who is so in love with us that it's impossible to stay away. I'm Christian because of Jesus, because in Jesus I encounter a love (and a God) that is constantly seeking us out. Jesus is love in action. The very act of the incarnation is God showing us a new way of living and being in relationship powered by love that is revealed in revolutionary relationship.

When we embody the love that Jesus modeled, we can't help but care for those on the margins. We must speak up and speak out against systems and institutions that oppress others. In the embodiment of this love, we recognize that our wellness is directly tied to the wellness of each member of humanity. When one is sick, we all are sick. When one suffers, we all suffer. When one is well, we all are well.

When we embody the love of God as revealed through the person of Jesus, we model this love with our whole being. To love big is to invite people to be made well, and this wellness has profound implications on our personal lives, our collective lives, and our world. In order to create wellness, we have to first address the symptoms and the causes of our diseased lives. Nothing can happen if we don't admit that we are wounded. Once we recognize and embrace our woundedness, we can begin the process of healing. This healing begins with falling in love with ourselves and a holistic practice of love, one that infiltrates our mind, heart, body, and soul. This leads us to live and love differently. We engage others in ways that bring about creativity and liberation, sustaining us on this journey. And these relationships bring about a deep, transformative healing. This process is difficult, but we don't do it alone. We do it in relationship with others, in revolutionary relationships.

This way of being challenges so many beliefs and ideas about how we should interact. This new world order moves us from being people who act upon others to being people who love one another, live with each other, and recognize our interconnectedness. When I love big, I recognize that the wellness I seek lies in how I love myself and how I love others. It lies in the wholeness of the community. It lies in the justice found when I take up the concerns and struggles of my neighbors. It lies in the original goodness that is reclaimed when we recognize ourselves and others as made in the Divine's image.

To love big is to recognize the inherent worth of everyone and to realize that the most important work to be done is the work of relationship. This leads to a fundamental shift in worldview so that all experience liberation today, here and now.

When we love big, we reflect the Divine Lover in our acts of creativity, in our work of liberation, and in how we sustain the relationships and the creation that God herself crafted. We love big when we fall in love with ourselves, rouse our minds, reform our bodies, and restore our hearts. We love big when we engage in revolutionary relationships and seek holistic healing, as individuals and as a community. To love big is to remember the beginning of our story, a story that reflects a God in revolutionary relationship, forming creation to experience and reciprocate love that leads to restoration, healing, and wholeness.

ACKNOWLEDGMENTS

I am a firm believer in village mentality. I am who I am and I'm am able to do what I do and show up how I show up because of the village that supports me. I would not have written this book without this village.

The Fortress Press team, especially Lisa my editor, who I am sure wanted to pull her hair out working with me but accompanied me from start to finish. This was the hardest thing I've ever done, and she made me better.

Dawn, who is the sweetest, kindest, and most supportive person I've met. She has been a wonderful thinking partner and constant encourager. She believed in *Love Big* before I did.

Kristen and Monica were the first readers of this book and provided editorial feedback. Their excitement about the book made me less afraid of its eventual release.

Austin served as a writing coach and pushed me to go beyond what I wrote to uncover the stories and lessons within me to share with readers.

ACKNOWLEDGMENTS

My roomie and life-long friend Beth, who sees me, knows me, and loves me unconditionally. She is the organizer of the chaos that is my life and has encouraged me through this book-writing process and beyond. She sat with me while I cried, wrote, procrastinated, planned, and created what you now hold in your hands.

I am grateful for my family, who also double as my team. My dad handles my email communication. My mother does my bookkeeping. My brother is my strategic-thinking partner. This is our story, our lessons, our project. They taught me how to love big, and we practice it every day.

I am thankful for every youth, young adult, and family that I have had the absolute pleasure and honor to accompany at some point of their journey. I would not be who I am without the diverse relationships in my life, without those who have taught me simply by being in relationship with me. I have uncovered love through these relationships. Every person has poured life into me and helped me become who I am today. I am the *Love Big* coach because these folks loved me to life. And for that, I am forever grateful.

NOTES

Introduction

1. Martin Luther King Jr., "Love, Law, and Civil Disobedience," in *A Testament of Hope: The Essential Writings and Speeches of Martin Luther King Jr.*, ed. James M. Washington (New York: HarperCollins, 1990), 51.

Chapter 1

1. Genesis 1:26–27 NRSV, emphasis added.
2. Randy Shilts, *The Mayor of Castro Street: The Life and Times of Harvey Milk* (New York: St. Martin's, 1982), 367.

Chapter 2

1. Brené Brown, *I Thought It Was Just Me (But It Isn't): Making the Journey from "What Will People Think?" to "I Am Enough"* (New York: Penguin Random House, 2007), xxiii–xxiv.
2. William H. Frey, "The New Great Migration: Black Americans' Return to the South, 1965–2000," Brookings Institution, May 1, 2004, https://tinyurl.com/yb43rjm5. The earlier move was termed the Great Migration—the period after the Civil War and post-Reconstruction when over six

million Blacks moved from southern states to the Northeast, Midwest, and West.

3. Kahlil Gibran, *The Prophet* (Mumbai: Shree Book Centre, 2006), 20.

4. *Sex and the City*, season 6, episode 20, "An American Girl in Paris: Part Deux," directed by Tim Van Patten, aired February 22, 2004 on HBO.

5. Matthew 22:36–40 NRSV, emphasis added.

6. Brené Brown, "The Power of Vulnerability," TEDx, June 2010, https://tinyurl.com/k5y5k2d.

Chapter 3

1. Henry David Thoreau, *A Week on the Concord and Merrimack Rivers* (Boston: James R. Osgood, 1873), 298.

2. Glocal Events are sponsored by the Evangelical Lutheran Church in America (ELCA) and equip folks for God's work in global and local realities, as well as their "glocal" intersections. At these events, participants consider the questions "What is mission?" and "Who is the neighbor?" For more information visit www.elca.org/glocal.

3. Antonio Machado, "One Word," trans. Robert Bly, Monasteries of the Heart, August 17, 2012, https://tinyurl.com/y8hzcbk5.

4. Frederick Douglass, "Southern Barbarism," in *The Life and Writings of Frederick Douglass*, ed. Philip Foner, vol. 4 (New York: International Publishers, 1950), 434.

5. Martin Luther King Jr., "Appendix: The Text of the 'Letter from Birmingham Jail,'" in *Gospel of Freedom: Martin Luther King Jr.'s Letter from Birmingham Jail and the Struggle That Changed a Nation*, by Jonathan Rieder (New York: Bloomsbury, 2013), 170.

6. Aboriginal activist groups, Queensland, 1970s.

Chapter 4

1. bell hooks, *All about Love: New Visions* (New York: HarperCollins), x.
2. Ntozake Shange, *For Colored Girls Who Have Considered Suicide / When the Rainbow Is Enuf* (New York: Scribner Poetry, 1997), 63.

Chapter 5

1. Nayyirah Waheed, "Starting," in *Salt* (n.p.: self-published, 2013), 145.

Chapter 6

1. Zora Neale Hurston, *Their Eyes Were Watching God* (Philadelphia: Lippincott, 1937), 192.
2. Deuteronomy 6:45 NIV.
3. W. E. B. Du Bois, *The Souls of Black Folk* (New York: Penguin, 1989), 5.

Chapter 7

1. Richard Rohr, *The Divine Dance: The Trinity and Your Transformation* (New Kensington, PA: Whitaker House, 2016).
2. Concept introduced to me by Father Jacob Breeze, pastor of Holy Family HTX in Houston, Texas.
3. I would recommend all of Brené Brown's work, but especially *The Gifts of Imperfection* (Center City, MN: Hazelden, 2010); "The Power of Vulnerability," TEDxHouston, 20:13, June 2010, https://tinyurl.com/oc4brbl; and her SuperSoul Sunday conversations with Oprah.

Chapter 8

1. Mark Hyman, MD, "The key to creating health is figuring out the cause of the problem and then providing the right conditions for the body and soul to thrive," Facebook, February 1, 2017, https://tinyurl.com/y96697mw.
2. WoundSource Editors, "The Four Stages of Wound Healing," WoundSource (blog), April 28, 2016, https://tinyurl.com/ybmu5xk3.
3. bell hooks, "A Chat with the Author of 'All about Love: New Visions,'" Chat Books, CNN.com, February 17, 2000, https://tinyurl.com/y7m4lphr.